By Christy Feinberg

Dedication

To those who see an artist's palette in a sunset. To those who hear a symphony in the chirps and squawks along a nature trail. And to those who feel a sugary spa when sinking your toes into the sand.

Life is short ... Live Like a Tourist.

Table of Contents

Live like a Tourist ... in Museums and Galleries

Live like a Tourist ... with Animals

Live like a Tourist ... while Exploring

Live Like A Tourist

Live like a Tourist … on an Adventure

Live like a Tourist … in the Great Outdoors

Live like a Tourist … during Happy Hour

Live Like A Tourist

... In Museums and Galleries

Bailey-Matthews National Shell Museum, Sanibel Island

I'm pretty familiar with cockles and various pen shells, but I don't think I've seen a half-naked one.

And that's a sentence I never expected to write, but that's what happens when you visit the Bailey-Matthews National Shell Museum on Sanibel Island. You're

probably familiar with the Florida prickly cockle as well, since it is a common shell found on Southwest Florida beaches.

The Florida prickly cockle is usually, "creamy-white to tawny-gray, with yellowish, orange, brownish and/or purplish patches," according to the shell museum's website. "Internally bright salmon, reddish, and/or purple. Albinistic specimens are sometimes found on the barrier islands."

The Bailey-Matthews National Shell Museum, celebrating its 20th anniversary in 2015, is the only museum in the country dedicated to shells and their mollusks.

The shell museum boasts more than 30 permanent exhibits, educating visitors about shells around the world and in our backyard. For example, one of the largest mollusks — the Queen Helmet — can be found in the Atlantic and Gulf of Mexico. The one on display at the shell museum is 15 inches.

One of the most beautiful exhibits is the Sailor's Valentines, which are elaborate shell-decorated boxes that were sold to sailors to give to their loved ones. One of the Sailor's Valentines on display by Sanibel resident Bert Porreca was featured on the "CBS News Sunday Morning."

Another interesting, yet frightening exhibit, informs visitors that some shells, while beautiful, also can be dangerous.

"Among the several hundred kinds of cone shells found in the warm seas of the world, five have killed humans," states the

Live Like A Tourist ... in Museums and Galleries

exhibit. "These small carnivorous snails feed on either worms, other snails or on small fish. When carelessly handled, five species from the southwest Pacific have killed several shell collectors. The injected venom is a strong neurotoxin causing death within a few hours."

Whoa! Imagine that obituary: John Smith died Sunday after being killed by a... shell. (Mental note: Add shells to the list of things I fear.)

"In Florida, the Alphabet Cone has caused painful stings, but no known deaths have been reported in Atlantic waters." (Second mental note: Lower shells on that list. Keep snakes, dart frogs, puffer fish, Tse Tse fly and polar bears at the top.)

The museum is packed with interesting exhibits, some of which are hands-on or interactive. There is a Children's Learning Lab as well where kids can play games and get their hands wet in a touch tank.

If You Go

Where: The Bailey-Matthews National Shell Museum 3075 Sanibel-Captiva Road, Sanibel
More info: 239-395-2233 or *www.shellmuseum.org*

In addition, Daily Tank Talks take place at 11:30 a.m. and 3:30 p.m. each day. These are kid-friendly and interesting for adults as well. At 1:30 p.m., another live lecture or event takes place and that topic varies by the day.

The gift shop at the Bailey-Matthews National Shell Museum is a great place to find unique shell-related gifts.

The shell museum is not a full-day adventure. Spend the day on Sanibel Island and explore the J.N. Ding Darling National Wildlife Refuge. Don't go on a Friday, however, as the famous Wildlife Drive is closed that day.

Since you're going to the shell museum, you'll probably want to go to the beach and find some shells of your own.

The shell museum provides the following tips for finding the shells:

- The best time is 90 minutes before low tide until 90 minutes after low tide.
- The best days are when a full moon and a new moon occurs, or after a storm.
- Try walking in a zig-zag fashion by starting at the high-tide line, going to the surf line and back again.

Remember: Don't take any live shells.

Just be sure to stretch before you start the "Sanibel Stoop." You don't want to throw out your back at the excitement of finding a half-naked pen shell or a pretty prickly cockle.

Boca Grande Lighthouse, Gasparilla Island

I'd forgotten how the brilliant, Crayola-colored waters could instantly slow my heart rate like a vacation on a Caribbean island.

When I first moved to Southwest Florida in 2000, I usually spent at least one day a month on a Gasparilla Island beach. Then, I would grab lunch or ice cream in Boca Grande.

Slowly over the years, I began to live less like a tourist and more like a resident.

It's easy to get caught up in the craziness of bills, house chores, yard work, etc. It's easy to forget that we live in one of the most beautiful vacation spots in the country.

I returned to the island that once served as my own personal vacation getaway to visit the Port Boca Grande Lighthouse Museum (commonly called the Boca Grande Lighthouse).

During season, 200 to 300 visitors travel through the lighthouse each day, said Amanda Pearsall, executive assistant.

Sometimes people confuse the two lighthouses (and by sometimes, I mean I once did).

The skinny white one, typically the first one seen on the island, is called the Rear Range Light. Its light is visible for nine miles.

The Boca Grande Lighthouse is the square-ish, house-like one at the south end of the island. It was built in 1890 and placed on the National Register of Historic Places 100 years later.

Live Like A Tourist ... in **Museums and Galleries**

Captains could tell the two lighthouses apart by their different flashing sequences.

As you enter the museum, you immediately learn about the history of Florida. Exhibits detail the Calusa and Spanish histories here.

There are collections of tools, shells and fossils, in addition to historical summaries of fishing, phosphate mining and living in Boca Grande.

For example, did you know that the Boca Grande School's football team (known as the Tarpons) won the state championship in 1938? I thought the football-powerhouse Tarpons were at Charlotte High.

Did you know that the school's basketball team had to travel by boat or ferry for away games? That would make for a long ride home if they lost and it was raining.

The island also played an interesting but little-known role in World War II. For example, did you know that German subs sank more than 100 allied ships in the Gulf of Mexico during the summer of 1942? Neither did I.

Of course there are historical summaries about the island's two lighthouses as well, but I don't want to spoil everything. The suggested donation is well worth the price of entry into the lighthouse museum.

Pearsall has been working for almost two years at the picturesque beach-front lighthouse.

"The view's not bad," she joked. "I learn something every day."

The museum's last room is a small but impressive gift shop. There are great children's books on sea life and Florida, jewelry, ornaments and other souvenirs.

When leaving, be sure to drive back through the downtown and stop for ice cream at the Pink Pony. Remember, there's no dieting on vacation. And we need to live a little more like tourists every now and then.

If You Go

Where: Inside Gasparilla Island State Park, 880 Belcher Road, Boca Grande
Tip: Don't forget to bring cash for the toll bridge and for entry into the state park.
More info: 941-964-0060

Calusa Nature Center and Planetarium, Fort Myers

A decades-long mystery may have been solved during a trip to the Calusa Nature Center & Planetarium.

What is Jabba the Hutt?

Surely there's a slug in his family tree (probably a pretty close relative). But as I walked up to a cage containing a slimy-looking, flabby troublemaker, I realized this was the closest I have ever been to Jabba the Hutt. Thus, I discovered that Jabba the Hutt must be related to an Argentine red tegu.

A te-what?

The Argentine red tegu, which grows to an average of 4 feet, is one of many critters on display at the Calusa Nature Center and Planetarium in Fort Myers.

The 105-acre site, located just off the Colonial Boulevard exit of Interstate 75, offers something for everyone.

Inside the main building at the Nature Center, visitors will learn about Florida's wildlife through exhibits as well as through live animals. Before you go, check the calendar online: www.calusanature.org/Calendar.html.

"I love it here," said education coordinator Victoria Menszak, who introduced guests to a red tail boa and a cane toad.

There are several rooms of wildlife — each with signs containing information  about the animals while educating visitors as to which critters are native to the region. For example, the Brooks king snake is native to Florida. It eats other snakes, making it my favorite snake. (That doesn't mean I want to hold one or see one near my house.)

Live Like A Tourist ... in Museums and Galleries

Now, if the Brooks king snake could eat the Burmese python, which is not native, that could solve a few problems for South Florida. But the Burmese python is twice the size (or more) of a Brooks king snake, making it an unlikely underdog-wins story.

There also are exhibits teaching guests about endangered species such as manatees and sea turtles.

Visitors can also learn about wildlife outside at the Audubon Aviary, which opened in 1981. The staff cares for injured eagles, hawks and other birds. More than 100 birds call the aviary home as they cannot be released into the wild.

There are three nature trails ranging from a third of a mile to one-and-a-third miles. Trail maps are available in the center.

After a stroll through the grounds, cool off in the planetarium, where several films are shown throughout the day. Again, check the calendar on the nature center's website for the movie listings.

The planetarium is the only one south of Bradenton, and it's a bit smaller... which leads to a very important tip. The Calusa Nature Center's Planetarium was a bit warm

If You Go

Where: Calusa Nature Center and Planetarium, 3450 Ortiz Ave., Fort Myers
More info:
www.calusanature.org or
239-275-3435

the day I went. (The one at the South Florida Museum was chilly.) If you are in a warm, small theater with comfortable chairs, guess what happens? Someone will fall asleep (not me). And yes, your snores can be heard over the audio.

It's hard not to compare the Calusa Nature Center and South Florida Museum, since they both have planetariums (the only ones in Southwest Florida). The Nature Center may be better for younger kids and for those who live closer to Fort Myers. The Bradenton-based museum is larger and geared toward older kids and adults.

The Calusa Nature Center and Planetarium is a great place to take kids who will enjoy seeing live animals, walking nature trails and learning about stars.

There is a small gift shop in the main building. There is no food served, but there are plenty of restaurants nearby.

Chihuly Collection, St. Petersburg

The red, blue, green and yellow lights turned ordinary glass into living, breathing, twinkling ornaments on a Christmas tree.

These were the ornaments I could stare at for hours as they changed in color with each passing shadow, setting sun, or gentle jiggle from the vibrations of excited little feet running by the tree. I appreciated glass art, but I had no idea how large, colorful, ornate and magnificent it could be until I saw the works of Dale Chihuly. The Morean Arts Center in St. Petersburg offers a permanent collection of Chihuly's pieces, which cannot be appreciated fully from photographs.

The Chihuly Collection, located separately from the Morean Arts Center, is an experience — especially for someone with little to no knowledge of Dale Chihuly or glass art.

Chihuly graduated in 1965 from the University of Washington, where he studied interior design. He then enrolled at the University of Wisconsin, which was the first glass program in the country, according to his website.

"He continued his studies at the Rhode Island School of Design, where he later established the glass program and taught for more than a decade," states his website, *www.chihuly.com*. "In 1968, after receiving a Fulbright Fellowship, he went to work

Live Like A Tourist ... in Museums and Galleries

at the Venini glass factory in Venice, Italy. There he observed the team approach to blowing glass, which is critical to the way he works today."

Chihuly returned to Washington, where he co-founded the Pilchuck Glass School.

His pieces can be seen in museums, galleries, libraries, resorts and even at the Bellagio in Las Vegas, where the chandelier called "Fiori di Como," with 2,000 hand-blown glass blossoms, adorns the lobby ceiling.

The Chihuly Collection in St. Petersburg houses the room-sized "Float Boat" sculpture. In layman's terms, it's a large boat filled with glass orbs of varying sizes on a mirror. It's simply stunning. The colorful balls bounce to life against the black backdrop, providing a dream-like, stress-erased world, where whatever you wish truly may float your boat.

The collection also houses extraordinary chandeliers — "Azul de Medianoche Chandelier" and "Ruby Red Icicle Chandelier" — that are so detailed you can't help but creep closer to inspect the lines, curves, clarity, etc. Unlike a lot of galleries or museums, you can get close enough to touch — but don't.

Be sure to stop by the gift shops at the Chihuly Collection on Beach Drive, and at the Morean Arts Center on Central Avenue. There are unique gifts made by local artists at the Arts Center, and plenty of Chihuly items at the Beach Drive site.

The Chihuly Collection also is located near the St. Petersburg Museum of History and the Dali Museum.

If You Go

Where: Chihuly Collection, 400 Beach Drive NE, St. Petersburg
More info:
www.moreanartscenter.org
or 727-896-4527

Crowley Museum and Nature Center, Sarasota

Those who are into history, birding and hiking can satisfy all three areas of interest by visiting the Crowley Museum and Nature Center in Sarasota.

Crowley occupies 191 acres of various habitats and easy-to-navigate hiking trails.

"John Crowley, the original pioneer settler on this land, was a blacksmith and farmer and rancher," states the website.

Guests are provided with an informative brochure/map/historical/wildlife guide.

The first place to begin is the boardwalk trail, where visitors may see birds, butterflies, alligators, turtles and other wildlife. It's a half-mile boardwalk that leads to the Selby Tower. The word "tower" is a little misleading. I wasn't expecting Bok Tower, but I was expecting something a little taller than a few feet off the ground. Nonetheless, it provides an elevated view and a shaded area to look for birds, alligators, otters, etc. The informational guide will teach you about lubber grasshoppers, poison ivy (which I can never spot), red maple, golden silk spiders, panthers, and other flora and fauna.

The boardwalk is easy to traverse.

The Children's Discovery Path also is easy to walk and informational. It's a great place for kids to burn off some

Live Like A Tourist ... in **Museums and Galleries**

afternoon sugar while learning about local critters. The path has five distinct areas designed for hands-on education about birds of prey, gopher tortoise, spiders, bats and panthers. For example, kids (or grown-up kids) can soar like an eagle on a little zip-line/swing or climb around a rope-made web like a spider.

The path is only three-eighths of a mile, so it's easy for little ones who tire sooner than expected. Of course, that means it's less terrain for you to be carrying a child on your back or shoulders.

In addition to trails, be sure to stop at the Tatum-Rawls House (circa 1888-1892).

"One of the oldest examples of rural architecture in Sarasota County, it was donated to Crowley by the Albritton family in 1996," states the brochure. That year, it was moved from its original site near Proctor Road to the Crowley Museum and Nature Center. It took five years and $100,000 to restore it, states Crowley's website.

Crowley also offers a Homestead Cabin, Pioneer Museum (designed to look like the one Crowley ran at the corner of Myakka and Rawls roads), Sugar Cane Mill and Tatum Ridge School House, which was closed in 1941.

There is a small gift shop as well with affordable prices.

Crowley offers a variety of youth programs. It would make a great place for field trips, and information about such programs is available on its website: *http://crowleyfl.org/programs/youth-programs*. It also provides events throughout the year such as full-moon walks, camp-outs and classes.

Crowley is near Myakka River State Park, so it's possible to explore both in one day.

The Dali Museum,
St. Petersburg

Faces melt. Seashells occupy brains. And, somehow, Abraham Lincoln magically appears.

Walking around the Dali Museum in St. Petersburg is like taking a stroll inside Salvador Dali's mind, though thankfully there are exits back to reality.

The museum itself, reflects Dali in its architecture: functional versus unexpected.

"Designed by architect Yann Weymouth of HOK, the new building combines the rational with the fantastical: a simple rectangle with 18-inch thick hurricane-proof walls out of which erupts a large free-form geodesic glass bubble known as the 'enigma,'" according to *www.thedali.org*. "The 'enigma,' which is made up of 1,062 triangular pieces of glass, stands 75 feet at its tallest point, a 21st century homage to the dome that adorns Dali's museum in Spain."

Inside the museum is a narrow, spiral staircase designed to look like "Dali's obsession with spirals and the double helical shape of the DNA molecule," states *www.thedali.org*. If you are capable of taking stairs, don't skip these steps. It's one of the most unique staircases you'll ever climb.

Live Like A Tourist ... in **Museums and Galleries**

The Dali Museum is filled with his work that spans his early years as an art student in Spain through his adult years.

Part of the admission price includes the use of an audio guide unit. Don't miss out on this either. The audio guide tour provides additional information about Dali than is available on signs. You will notice that there are two different numbers and symbols for the audio guide by some pieces of Dali's art. One is the serious, straight-forward information. The other, denoted by the mustache symbol, is geared to kids between the ages of 5 and 13. (Inside tip: Play the mustache numbers too. You will learn fun, entertaining information about Dali such as how "he drove his teachers crazy" and what he did to be the center of attention.)

If You Go

Where: The Dali Museum, One Dali Blvd., St. Petersburg
More info: 727-823-3767 or *http://thedali.org/home.php*

The museum also offers free docent tours throughout the day, though these can be crowded.

The following are just some of Dali's amazing artwork on display:
- "Santiago El Grande," a 1957 painting of the Patron Saint of Spain.
- "The Average Bureaucrat," a 1930 painting of his father.
- "Galacidalacidesoxyribonucleicacid," an incredible 1963 mural.
- "The Discovery of America by Christopher Columbus," a 1958-1959 mural.
- "Gala Contemplating the Mediterranean Sea which at 20 Meters Becomes the Portrait Abraham Lincoln," a 1976 remarkable piece that has to be seen in person.

The museum offers a large gift shop filled with Dali memorabilia, which includes shirts, jewelry, prints, puzzles and other one-of-a-kind gifts.

There is a small restaurant, Cafe Gala, named after Dali's wife. There, you can order light Spanish foods.

Expect to spend at least two hours (may take longer if there are lots of crowds or school groups) exploring the museum and the grounds, which are impeccably landscaped and include a maze that must be explored.

Edison & Ford Winter Estates, Fort Myers

Florida, with its newish history, its transient population and its propensity to color most everything in hues of weirdness, isn't the state most immediately thought of as a place of significance in the story of America.

Sure, there's Ponce de Leon. Sure, there are some interesting Cuban connections. Sure, there are always some strange footnote attached to many chapters on elections.

But there's a place right here in Southwest Florida where two men's footprints turned 20 acres of soil, rich with their American ingenuity, into a historical landmark — the Edison & Ford Winter Estates.

Thomas Edison and Henry Ford, two of the greatest brains in American history, escaped the northern winters by vacationing along the Caloosahatchee River in Fort Myers. Edison bought land in 1885 and built his house in 1886. He and his wife, Mina, spent time at the Fort Myers estate until Mina deeded it to the city for $1 in 1947. Ford bought his home in 1916.

It's quite remarkable to imagine the two brilliant men watching sunsets, bouncing around ideas and borrowing cups of milk from each other. OK, they probably didn't do that last one.

Christmas is an especially beautiful time of year to visit the estates, which are impeccably decorated. The inside of Edison's home is adorned with Christmas decorations accurate to the first half of the 1900s. The dining room table is set to reflect Mina Edison's Christmas Eve dinner, which included oysters and, specifically, good applesauce.

There are various tour options. First-timers may want to consider the Complete Estates Tour, which "offers a complete orientation and a self-guided audio tour of the historic homes, gardens and laboratory of the Edison and Ford families as well as the museum. The museum contains an impressive collection of inventions, artifacts and special exhibits," states the website.

Audio wands are available in several different languages.

The museum is overwhelming in a good way. It's amazing to see Edison's inventions: the phonograph, talking doll, movie-making equipment, dictating machine, etc. It's also remarkable to walk around and see the gardens, along with Edison's 1910 swimming pool.

It's recommended to give yourself at least three hours for a tour and to explore the grounds (I'd say give yourself at least four or five hours with a drink/meal break). There are benches scattered around for those who need to slow down or take a break.

There are more in-depth tours offered as well, including a behind-the-scenes tour and one that focuses on the beautiful gardens and specially grown plants (some of which Edison purposely planted for research).

Be sure to check out the gift shops and the Garden Shoppe.

If You Go

Where: Edison & Ford Winter
Estates, 2350 McGregor Blvd.,
Fort Myers
Tips: Wear comfortable shoes as
the tour is about a mile
More info: 239-334-7419 or
www.edisonfordwinterestates.org

Florida Holocaust Museum, St. Petersburg

I call it the Boxcar Theory.

Maybe it's not an original thought. Maybe somebody else coined the phrase. Doesn't really matter.

A few years ago, I visited the Florida Holocaust Museum in St. Petersburg. I was single, in my 20s, and going through "problems" no one else had to endure because that's what you think when you spend too much time inside your head.

While walking around the museum, it came into view. The boxcar. Boxcar No. 113 069-5, specifically.

I stared.

The boxcar silenced the petty, silly, unimportant "problems" in my head.

The boxcar once carried 100 or so people at a time to concentration camps.

Live Like A Tourist ... **in Museums and Galleries**

It served as a cage, confining women, children, elderly, Jews, homosexuals, gypsies… people. It transported them in ways we might ship harvested fruits, allowing no room for the cargo to shift… or breathe.

I continued staring.

My "problems" suddenly amounted to a paltry pile of pebbles (if that). My worst day is still a good one.

That's the Boxcar Theory, though really it's just a reminder to put "problems" into a proper perspective.

I revisited the Florida Holocaust Museum and Boxcar No. 113 069-5, which is a permanent exhibit, "History, Heritage and Hope," and centerpiece of the museum. The boxcar sits on original railroad tracks from the Treblinka killing center in Poland.

If You Go

Where: Florida Holocaust Museum, 55 5th St. S., St. Petersburg
More info: *www.flholocaustmuseum.org* or 727-820-0100

While the boxcar attracts much attention because of its size and its significance, the museum is filled with other educational displays and moving exhibits.

Guests are provided with an audio wand, which allows visitors to tour the museum at their own pace. Also, if you missed a piece of information, you can simply type in the display number and listen again. It's a convenient way to tour a museum, which starts out introducing visitors to the history of hate and the rise of the Nazis.

There is a small theater where you can hear about Denmark's King Christian X, Oskar Schindler, Anne Frank's father and protectors along with others who did their parts to minimize the atrocities. There also is a wall honoring those who have shown courage and sacrifice.

Consider carving out about two hours to fully explore the museum. There is a gift shop with interesting books. There also are plenty of restaurants within walking distance before driving home.

Imaginarium Science Center, Fort Myers

We watched a 3-D movie, met some critters, built roller coasters, played sports, found dinosaur bones and experienced a hurricane (sort of).

That's a lot of fun fora few dollars.

The Imaginarium Science Center in Fort Myers is a great place to take kids. Since my "children" walk on all fours, chase bunnies and perceive a door knock

as an invasion, I needed to find some upright-walking children to borrow (which sounds weird but showing up to Imaginarium with no kids might be even more creepy).

The Fritsch family kindly lent me 10-year-old Victor and 8-year-old Natalie (I've known the Fritsches for years so this is actually far less strange than it sounds).

Both Victor and Natalie are incredibly intelligent and polite, but they are still kids with active imaginations and genuine enthusiasm.

Immediately after paying the entry fee, we learned that a 3-D movie would be playing within a few minutes and the topic: penguins.

"That's my favorite animal," Natalie excitedly said while wearing a T-shirt that happened to have penguins on it.

We got our 3-D glasses and watched a 20-minute film about the lives of King Penguins on South Georgia Island, a sub-antarctic island.

After the film, Imaginarium offered Animal Encounters in the same theater.

Out came a creepy critter in need of moisturizer, which Victor immediately identified: a bearded dragon.

Live Like A Tourist ... in Museums and Galleries

"I want a bearded dragon and I'd name him Dave," Victor said.

The next animal was a tortoise, which prompted the Fritsch kids to announce they want turtles and they each had names picked out: Natalie selected Bob; Victor chose Franklin, or Frank for short.

The third animal was Natalie's worst nightmare: a big, squishy toad (she hates frogs/toads). She immediately fled her seat and found the farthest possible chair.

But the kids learned that this toad eats frogs, among other things.

"So it's a cannibal?" Victor asked. "He looks like a cannibal."

Victor then tried helping his sister by explaining that the toad eats frogs, and since she hates frogs, the toad is then her friend. When that didn't work, he offered her $1 if she would touch the toad.

"Seriously?" she asked him.

"Yes."

So she touched the toad and then reminded him several times how he owed her a dollar.

Neither had trouble touching the stingrays in one of the two Sea to See Touch Tanks. Guests are allowed to feel the smooth skin of stingrays several times a day. The other tank has starfish and even a flounder, which had tucked itself into the sand making it nearly invisible (although Victor spotted it easily).

There's another area of live animals as well, but the snakes, frogs, turtles, etc., are kept in cages (which is good because they have a poisonous dart frog — scary).

The main science room is really like a gym filled with toys and activities. Young kids likely have no idea they're really learning about Newton's Laws of Motion, physics, archaeology and even kinesiology.

Victor spent time building a roller coaster. Natalie and Victor enjoyed the Sporty Science Area where guests play simulated skills tests in the areas of soccer, hockey, basketball, football and baseball (OK, I did too). The two participated in an archaeological dig (fine, I did too). They really enjoyed seeing what 45 mph winds feels like in the Hurricane Experience (yup, I did too). In fact, we sat through the Hurricane Experience three times.

"Science is fun," Victor said.

It really is.

If You Go

Where: Imaginarium Science Center, 2000 Cranford Ave., Fort Myers
More info: 239-321-7420 or *i-sci.org*

Lovegrove Gallery and Gardens, Matlacha Island

Red mixed with blue creates purple… but not for Leoma Lovegrove.

The Lovegrove Gallery and Gardens is a must-see attraction in Matlacha, where visitors can glimpse the Skittles explosion of colors in a Wonka-like wonderland of curiosity and genius.

Leoma paints what she loves: Florida, patriotism, religion, music and, of course, The Beatles. In fact, she'll paint anything, including her shoes and the pants she once wore to the White House.

"I've never been afraid to throw paint anywhere," she said.

Many know Leoma from her exclusive collection at Bealls, where fans can purchase her artwork on clothing, dishes, bags, etc.

"What Bealls did for me is made me more mainstream," she said.

The woman who has painted for world and corporate leaders enjoys seeing people wearing her clothes.

"I still get a kick out of it," she said. "I'll be in Publix, hiding behind vegetables and taking a photo of someone."

The Gary, Ind., native studied at the Ringling College of Art and Design. She settled in Matlacha 18 years ago.

"When I moved here, it was like a fishermen's village," she said. "Now, our No. 1 industry is tourism."

The brightly colored Lovegrove Gallery and Gardens, in fact, received TripAdvisor Certificates of Excellence.

The gallery is filled with huge masterpieces few can afford. But she also creates clever letter-shaped pieces out of old Reader's Digest books and smaller pieces as well, so almost anyone can take home an original Leoma Lovegrove piece of art.

Leoma's gardens are a gorgeous, fun mix of nature and art — complete with a stage.

"We have music out there in the winter, and I paint onstage," she said.

The stage's backdrop, of course, is The Beatles.

Live Like A Tourist … in Museums and Galleries

"I started painting The Beatles maybe 15 years ago. … Their music made sense to me," she said. "Everybody loves them. I always have a big area for The Beatles."

She has heard that Ringo Starr has some of her art.

"But I don't know how to validate that," she said.

She does, however, know that her paintings are in presidential libraries.

President Jimmy Carter and his wife Rosalynn visited Leoma during the holidays in 2004, just a few months after Hurricane Charley.

"We got our gallery back together so quick," she said. "When they picked out our place, we offered them a private garden party.

"I painted his portrait and he accepted it out in the garden."

Where: Lovegrove Gallery and Gardens, 4637 Pine Island Road NW, Matlacha Island
More info: 239-283-6453 or *www.leomalovegrove.com*

That portrait now hangs in Carter's Presidential Library.

She went to the White House in 2008, during President George W. Bush's last term.

"Everyone came in wearing black, and I came in looking like an ornament," she said.

Her artwork has been displayed in Bush's Presidential Library, as well as in the windows of Rockefeller Center in New York. She also was commissioned to paint Richard Branson for his Virgin Airlines headquarters in London.

While her work is known around the globe, it may be her funky eyeglasses that most people recognize.

"I have about 20 pairs," she said. She has one pair that sparkles with 350 Swarovski crystals, which she wears after 5 p.m.

The pair of glasses, like every piece of art, has a story too.

Her mother Rosemary also was an artist.

"I originally bought them for my mother. She immediately put her prescription in them," she said.

Rosemary became ill and since has passed away.

"I put my prescription in them," Leoma said.

Now, those glasses, along with her brilliant paintings, have made Leoma Lovegrove an artistic icon.

A trip to Lovegrove Gallery and Gardens can be a full day of fun. There are several cute, local stores and galleries within walking distance, as well as restaurants.

Military Heritage Museum, Punta Gorda

There are places our grandparents, parents, siblings, neighbors and friends have been that we don't want to imagine: a crowded Higgins Boat in rough seas, a cramped bamboo cage in Vietnam, an Afghan street pockmarked with disguised roadside bombs.

These are just some of the places the bravest among us have endured as military veterans of our great country.

It's important to remember not only what happened but also who it happened to — and not just for a few days around Veterans Day and Memorial Day.

The Military Heritage Museum in Punta Gorda is free and open seven days a week, allowing all of us an opportunity to step inside and honor our veterans.

The museum has been located inside its current site near the entrance of Fishermen's Village since 2007 and since has expanded, opening up almost 300 additional square feet, said Kim Lovejoy, executive director of the museum.

There are uniforms, medals, letters, flags and weapons from various wars and conflicts. There is a display on one wall of 10 U.S. Army uniforms. There also is a case of firearms.

One of the most eye-catching exhibits is the bamboo cage, which is a replica of the ones used to hold U.S. prisoners of war

Live Like A Tourist ... **in Museums and Galleries**

captured in Vietnam. Capt. Luis Chirichigno, of Southwest Florida, spent eight months in such a cage before being transferred to Hanoi Hilton.

"While in captivity, it was the message his former football coach, Bear Bryant, gave to the team that he credits for giving him the strength to survive his ordeal: 'Never give up,'" states one of the explanatory signs in the museum.

Chirichigno endured a total of 3 ½ years as a prisoner of war. He later donated his pink-striped POW uniform and Ho Chi Minh sandals to the Military Heritage Museum, which are on display near the bamboo cage.

There's something at the museum that delivers more of an impact than the bamboo cage, photographs or the model airplanes. It's the volunteers, many of whom are veterans willing to share their stories.

"These days the bulk are Vietnam," Kim said.

Every day, we're losing these incredible men and women.

For example: Retired Brig. Gen. J. Robinson Risner died at the age of 88. He spent seven years, four months and 27 days as the highest-ranking American prisoner of war in Vietnam, according to the Los Angeles Times.

The U.S. Census reported that Charlotte County has 25,669 veterans, about 16 percent of its total population. In Sarasota, the Census reported 48,765 veterans or 12.6 percent of the county's population.

The Military Heritage Museum, which is now about 2,400 square feet, is expanding to include a sitting area and library.

"We want to make it available for students," Kim said.

The museum has a gift shop as well that includes books, hats and other military items. Admission is free, but donations are greatly appreciated.

If You Go

Where: Military Heritage Museum, inside Fishermen's Village, 1200 W. Retta Esplanade, Punta Gorda
More info: *www.freedomisntfree.org* or 941-575-9002

Muscle Car City Museum, Punta Gorda

Angel Alejandro took four young relatives to Muscle Car City in Punta Gorda.

The five of them walked around, looking at Camaros and Corvettes, and carrying on in-depth automotive conversations.

"I love it," said Angel, of New Jersey.

Each of the boys had a favorite car.

- Rafael Leroux, 14, of Winter Haven, Fla.: 1969 Camaro SS
- Ryan Ruiz, 11, of New Jersey: 1971 Chevelle
- Kyle Alejandro, 11, of New Jersey: 1969 Camaro Copo (orange)
- Aaron Ruiz, 14, of New Jersey: 1969 Camaro SS

The boys, wide-eyed and smiling, weren't the only ones walking around Muscle Car City like… well… a group of boys in a 99,000-square-foot museum filled with more than 200 cars.

Let me take a moment to confess something: I'm not a car nut. I can't change my own oil. I can't even change a tire. I refer to car parts as "shiny thingies," "wobble bobbles," and "chug chuggers."

Despite my inability to tell the difference between a Firebird and a Thunderbird, I felt welcomed at Muscle Car City. I also felt as wide-eyed as those boys

— after all, it doesn't require a degree in "wobble chuggers" to appreciate the collection of amazing cars.

As soon as you walk into the museum, it's overwhelming. You are greeted by a line of Corvettes on your right as soon as you open the door. Several old, regal cars stand as reminders of the 1920s and 1930s on the left side of the aisle.

All of these cars belong to one man: Rick Treworgy.

And Mark Skinner is lucky enough to be at Muscle Car City almost every day.

If You Go

Where: Muscle Car City Museum, 3811 Tamiami Trail, Punta Gorda. The Museum is expected to relocate to 10175 Tamiami Trail, in Punta Gorda, in the spring of 2016 so be sure to check the website or call ahead of your visit.

More info: 941-575-5959 or *http://musclecarcity.net*

Tips: Bring a camera. Still photos are allowed, but video is not. Also, don't wear big chains or big, long-strapped purses that will smack or scratch a car if you get close.

"It's like a dream job," Mark said.

Mark has worked at Muscle Car City for years. He works in maintenance, but he also gladly provides helpful assistance or interesting information about the cars.

"It's a pretty impressive collection," Mark said. "Everything in here will start and drive."

There are about 230 cars (mostly Chevrolets) on display at a time, and 67 of those are Corvettes, Mark said. Visitors also can see Monte Carlos, Camaros, Impalas and El Caminos.

"You can usually tell how old a person is by where they gravitate to," he said.

Famous visitors include Baseball Hall of Famer Reggie Jackson; Chip Foose, from "Overhaulin'"; and George Barris, creator of the 1966 TV Batmobile.

Cathy and Mark Fitzpatrick of Port Charlotte visited the museum for the first time.

"We think it's fantastic," Cathy said.

"I'm a Chevy guy," Mark said. "My dream cars are station wagons."

The museum also offers a diner, which you can go to without paying the admission price. The diner's decor reflects the cruising music playing throughout the old Walmart building with its black and white checkered floor, and red and black tables and booths.

Just like the boys visiting, I too picked out my favorite car: The pretty blue 1954 Corvette… not a bad pick for a girl who can't find a car's dipstick.

Museum of Science and Industry (MOSI), Tampa

The Museum of Science and Industry, MOSI for short, offers a full day of Sheldon Cooper-loving fun (and you don't have to be a "Big Bang Theory" fan or a science geek to have a good time).

The 10,000-square-foot "Disasterville" exhibit allows visitors to quasi-experience a tornado, wildfire, earthquake and hurricane. The tornado puts you

in a basement setting to ride out the fierce winds. The wildfire allows you to actually smell the blaze and see the emergency officials quickly responding. The earthquake simulates the shaking ground, though there are handrails so you can hold on safely.

But the hurricane... oh that dastardly large natural disaster... actually shows storm chaser video footage of Hurricane Charley hitting Punta Gorda. Needless to say, I didn't stay long in there. Been there, done that and got the T-shirt. (Isn't that what they say?) If you step into the hurricane tube, where you can feel 75-mph-plus winds, be sure to hold onto your hat, glasses and other belongings. Also, ladies and long-haired men, be ready to forfeit a good hair day if you step into the tube (and make sure you have a clip, hair tie or other way to contain your wild hair after the winds settle).

MOSI is packed with 400,000 square feet of entertaining education (or is it educational entertainment?).

It may be called "Kids in Charge," but there's plenty of fun for the young at heart in this 40,000-square-foot section of the museum. "Slippery Science," is one of the newer, cooler (pun intended) areas of the exhibit. It incorporates the Tampa Bay Lightning and the Tampa Bay Times Forum to teach about friction, physics, safety and reaction times.

"Mission: Moonbase" also is located in the "Kids in Charge" area, but adults can definitely participate. I successfully piloted a rover along the bumpy surface of the moon. There are many other space tasks visitors can attempt, but my rover-driver skills proved to be so brilliant I'm surprised NASA hasn't made contact yet.

If You Go

Where: MOSI, 4801 E. Fowler Ave., Tampa
More info: 813-987-6000 or *www.mosi.org*

Expect to spend at least an hour (likely more) in this area as there are so many interesting hands-on experiments.

At some point during your day, you'll want to sit down and relax. That should be the time for you to watch an IMAX documentary. Some ticket options include one IMAX. There is a concession area in the lobby of the IMAX, where guests can purchase popcorn, pretzels, candy and drinks.

In addition to the indoor exhibits and IMAX theater, the adventurous can fly down the zip-line or traverse the ropes course (extra charge).

Be sure to save some time to visit the gift shop and to explore the grounds, which includes the beautiful BioWorks Butterfly Garden.

Ringling Museum of Art, Sarasota

If you are an art connoisseur, you may want to carve out an entire day. If you are more like me (someone who can't stare at a painting for more than a few seconds), a half-day adventure is more likely, depending on the weather and how much time you spend strolling the spectacular gardens on the 66 acres of impeccably manicured grounds (more on that later).

The museum opened to the public more than 80 years ago.

Immediately upon entering the grounds, I paused at the beauty. I had heard it was beautiful, but this blew me away. One of the first stops along the stroll is 100-year-old Mable's Rose Garden.

Live Like A Tourist ... in **Museums and Galleries**

The garden, which is filled with varieties of roses and statues, is an Accredited Public Rose Garden by the American Rose Society.

Continue walking (or riding one of the free shuttles) by the majestic banyan trees and into the Secret Garden. It's a quiet area, subtly marked by graves: Ida Ringling North, John Ringing, Mable Burton Ringling. The headstones indicate the three were interred there June 4, 1991.

The 36,000-square-foot Ca' D'Zan, while not included in the free admission on Mondays, sits on the water as more of a castle than mansion. I definitely need to check out the art-filled 56 rooms on my next trip.

Also near the water is the Millennium Tree Trail, which is a newer addition to the property.

It was built in 2000 for the National Millennium Arbor Day Celebration and includes a variety of trees. The great thing about the trail is all the educational signage identifying trees. The signs also educate visitors as to how each tree grows in sun versus shade, and how fast each will grow. There are palms, pines and magnolias planted along the trail, but my favorite is the Gumbo Limbo because no other tree is as fun to say.

After walking the grounds, I finally headed into the Museum of Art with its numerous galleries and exquisite courtyard. While I may not be an art collector or an art student, I certainly appreciated the incredible collections and exhibits.

For more on Ringling, go to *www.ringling.org.*

If You Go

Where: Ringling Museum of Art, 5401 Bay Shore Road, Sarasota
Discounts: *http://www.ringling. org/hours-admissions*
More info: *www.ringling.org* or 941-359-5700

Sarasota Classic Car Museum, Sarasota

I always imagined classy, old-school Hollywood stars to cruise around in fancy BMWs, Jaguars or Bentleys. Maybe something foreign like an Alfa Romeo? Or a James Bond-like Aston Martin?

The Sarasota Classic Car Museum has a few celebrities' vehicles in its collection.

There's John Lennon's 1965 Mercedes-Benz 230SL as well as his 1979 Mercedes-Benz 300TD.

There's the 1924 Rolls-Royce Silver Ghost owned by Sarasota residents John and Mable Ringling.

Then there's Katharine Hepburn's car... the unsuspecting, white patrol car. Yes, one of Hollywood's finest actresses rode around in a 1995 Ford Crown Victoria.

"The car was chauffeur-driven and dealer maintained," states the sign attached the car. "Well equipped with all significant accessories, she owned it for some nine years."

It's funny to think about Katharine Hepburn riding around in the back of a patrol car. While I have no idea if she actually rode in the backseat, I can confirm that her Crown Vic's backseat appeared to be far more comfortable than the usual cramped, caged-in area of a police officer's Crown Vic.

Katharine Hepburn supposedly said: "My greatest strength is common sense. I'm really a standard brand — like Campbell's tomato soup or Baker's chocolate." She could have added the brand Ford to that list.

That's one of the interesting things about the Sarasota Classic Car Museum — seeing the personalities in the cars. Who would have thought the Hollywood actress would own such a practical automobile? But that was Katharine Hepburn, a woman known for wearing jeans and no makeup in a glamorous world.

Then there's John Lennon. It wasn't surprising to see the young, wealthy music icon driving Mercedes Benz vehicles. Nor is it a shock to see the Ringlings owned a Rolls-Royce.

Herbert and Bob Horn opened the museum, then called the Horns' Cars of Yesterday, in 1953. The museum has changed

Live Like A Tourist ... in Museums and Galleries

hands a few times with Martin Godbey buying it most recently in 1997. The Sarasota Classic Car Museum claims to be the "second oldest continuously operating antique car museum in the nation" and the "nation's oldest continuously operating car museum," according to its website.

Regardless, it's an interesting way to escape an afternoon shower if you are at a Sarasota beach. Or, you can work it in with a day at the John and Mable Ringling Museum of Art, which is just across Tamiami Trail. Unless you are a car nut, don't expect to spend more than an hour or two at the car museum.

There are more than 75 vehicles on display (most of which were not owned by celebrities, but are unique nonetheless).

One of the first vehicles you will encounter is a 1905 Schacht, from Cincinnati. Only 713 were built, according to the informational sign.

Among the beauties: a 1957 Pontiac Bonneville (one of only 630), a 1993 Jaguar XJ220 (MSRP $706,000) and a 1972 IsoRivolta Varedo (only one produced), information provided by the museum. I had many "I'll take one of those" moments in the museum, but these three definitely stood out near the top of my list.

If You Go

Where: Sarasota Classic Car Museum, 5500 N. Tamiami Trail, Sarasota

More info: 941-355-6228 or *www.sarasotacarmuseum.org*

In addition to the classic autos, there also is an area with antique arcade games. There is a store attached to the museum as well, but don't expect to find the perfect souvenir or gift as the selection is small.

So the obvious question: Why would I go to a museum in Sarasota when there's a large car museum in Punta Gorda?

First, the Sarasota museum has a variety of cars: Fords, Jeeps, Jaguars, Bentleys, etc. Muscle Car City has more than 200 General Motors cars, including Corvettes from every year between 1954 and 1975. So that decision depends on your taste in cars.

Second, you can work in the Sarasota museum with a beach trip, Ringling museum visit, etc. Katharine Hepburn likely would appreciate the practicality of saving gas and combining a trip to see her Crown Vic with another attraction in Sarasota.

Solomon's Castle, Ona

I see empty dog food cans, beer bottles, soda cans, juice jugs and milk bottles in my recycling bin.

Howard Solomon might see an octopus window-washing team ("they really stick to it").

Solomon sees art and irony in everyday trash, and thus has created a fantastical wonderland on 90 acres in Hardee County known as Solomon's Castle.

That's right, he built a castle.

"I love it," said tour guide Cindy O'Connor. "I just love the place. It's unique."

To say the least.

Solomon started building the castle in 1972, but his interest in art started at a young age. He carved a truck out of wood at age 4. (You can see the truck during the tour, and it's shockingly accurate.)

In the 1960s, he sold his metal and wood sculptures in his galleries in Miami and the Bahamas, according to "The Castle in the Swamp," written by Solomon's wife, Peggy Reilly Solomon.

When the Solomons moved to Hardee County, they knew they would need a large space to house Howard's sculptures as well as an area for a workshop. Thus, they began building the castle that also serves as their home.

Solomon used aluminum newspaper press plates on the outside to give the castle its gray, metallic appearance.

More than 90 Solomon-made stained glass windows adorn the castle. Some of the windows are arranged by theme. There is a children's nursery rhyme section as well as one dedicated to the planets.

What may be more fascinating than a castle in a swamp is what's inside: an unbelievable collection of Solomon's art.

Solomon recycles trash into art. He uses car parts, beer cans, oil drums, wire hangers, wood scraps, etc. Even more remarkable than the art (if that's even possible), is Solomon's sense of humor. Pay special attention to the names of his pieces of art (example: WMD or Weapon of Mouse Destruction).

If You Go

Where: Solomon's Castle, 4533 Solomon Road, Ona

More info: *www.solomonscastle. org* or 863-494-6077

The pun-filled tour reflects Solomon's wit and Willy Wonka-esque imagination.

O'Connor introduced us to a sculpture called "Confusion." It was sent to Palm Beach County to vote, O'Connor said, referring to the 2000 presidential election.

"We call him Chad," she joked.

The tour includes a zoo-like experience. Well, not really, but Solomon did create a menagerie of animals made from 50 pounds of wire hangers.

Other treasures include:

- A 190-pound lion made from five oil drums.
- An elephant named "Jeb the Bushman."
- Several Picasso paintings replicated using wood scraps.
- Several Saturday Evening Post covers using wood scraps.
- A "Where's Waldo" chess set.

One of the most special parts of the tour includes part of the Solomons' living quarters.

After seeing how a "unique" man created an art-filled castle, I didn't expect to find this in his glass cupboard: bland, boring, ordinary oatmeal. I hope he at least sprinkles in some Gummy Bears or Junior Mints or caramel-coated thimbles.

Guests can spend a night in the castle in the Blue Moon Room.

"See what happens after dark… you never know," challenged O'Connor.

The tour ends at the Boat in the Moat restaurant, which is literally a boat in a moat built by Solomon, of course. It is three-quarters the size of the Santa Maria.

The restaurant is run by Solomon's daughter, Alane, and son-in-law, Dean. The food is excellent. I ate their tuna salad, which was served with chips and a side. I chose their special spinach casserole and I'm glad I did.

Exploring Solomon's castle shouldn't end at lunch. There are surprises around all over the 90 acres, including a replica of the Alamo (because why not?).

There also is a nature walk (good to do after lunch). The trail starts near the parking lots and winds around the castle, but watch out for the real alligator.

Solomon's Castle is a must-see for residents and visitors alike.

South Florida Museum, Bradenton

Many Very Eager Men Just Sat Up Naming Planets.
Many Very Eager Men Just Sat Up Nodding Plenty.
Many Very Eager Men Just Sat Up Needing Pizza.

Well it was something along those lines, but that's how I remembered the planets in the solar system as a kid. Then we learned that Pluto isn't a planet.

So I guess it's just now: Many Very Eager Men Just Sat Up Needing? I have a feeling that's not what's being taught now.

I had forgotten about my childhood fascination with all things "space" until I found myself sitting inside the Bishop Planetarium at the South Florida Museum in Bradenton.

The old manatee named Snooty may be the celebrity at the museum, but I could spend far more time in the planetarium (no offense, Snooty).

The South Florida Museum, one of the best in the region, is basically three museums under one roof. There's the main museum, which includes two stories of incredible galleries from the mastodon to a Mickey Mouse camera. There's the Parker Manatee Aquarium, where Snooty lives as the oldest known manatee in captivity. There's the planetarium, where various fascinating films are shown throughout the day.

Live Like A Tourist ... **in Museums and Galleries**

"I love the planetarium movies," said Bradenton resident Suzanne Smith. "I can see them over and over again."

I watched three films: "Extreme Planets," "Ultimate Universe," and "Two Small Pieces of Glass." There are additional shows at the planetarium as well, so be sure to check the schedule online.

Between shows, visit Snooty and see the trainers hand-feed him at various times throughout the day.

Marcus and Lindsay Verdu of Ontario couldn't wait to see Snooty.

"We're here to see the manatee," Lindsay said.

Snooty was born July 21, 1948, at the old Miami Aquarium, making him the first manatee known to have been born in captivity. He was relocated to Bradenton in 1949.

The main museum area is far larger with many more exhibits than expected.

On the first floor, you can learn what mastodons likely ate and learn why dinosaurs never roamed these parts of Florida. You can also see fossils and artifacts from early Floridians. In addition, you'll find the underwater viewing area of the aquarium, the Spanish Plaza, 1500s Spanish Home and Spanish Chapel.

There are about 10 galleries on the second floor, which are equally if not more fascinating than those on the first floor. Exhibits include information about mangroves, the Manatee River and living in the area as it has developed. One of the more interesting parts is the Medical Gallery, where you can see old medical tools and displays of an operating room, pharmacy and dental office.

Be sure to save time for the museum shop before you leave. It's a great place for books, shirts, stuffed animals, toys, decorations and lots of Snooty attire, of course.

Southwest Florida Military Museum and Library, Cape Coral

There are 1.6 million stories belonging to the 1.6 million veterans living in Florida.

That's a lot of stories... many of which will remain untold.

There are, however, lots of known stories of battles fought and won, of days spent weathering smothering tropical heat or crippling frozen temperatures, and of friends, brothers, sons who never came home.

There are flags — some of them ours and some of them our enemies' — that made their way back to the States. There are canteens, rifles, uniforms and letters as well.

To honor the 1.6 million Florida veterans, there are dozens of military museums scattered across the state.

The closest one, the Military Heritage Museum in Punta Gorda, displays more than 30,000 items from a variety of conflicts and wars. The museum is free (donations appreciated) and open seven days a week in Fishermen's Village. It's a well-organized museum filled with informational and interesting exhibits.

If you are in the Cape Coral area, be sure to stop by another museum honoring our finest Floridians. The Southwest Florida Military Museum & Library occupies 34,000 square feet, where visitors can see beautiful displays and military artifacts.

Live Like A Tourist ... in **Museums and Galleries**

The museum is organized chronologically, starting with the Revolutionary War and progressing into the ongoing conflicts in the Middle East. There are additional exhibits about the Cold War, space exploration and the Kennedy assassination as well.

In the Civil War section, guests can expect to see a piece of a tree that still contains a cannonball and musket ball from the Civil War. Other artifacts from that era include a water keg, pistols and a cannonball. There also is a piece of a slave restraint used at a plantation in Virginia. That might have been one of the more haunting pieces of history in the museum.

There are dozens of uniforms from the various branches and eras, along with weapons and medals.

Some of the more unusual artifacts include: a phone from the Reichstag in Germany, a WWII-era baseball glove, a prayer book from WWI, a first aid kit from WWII, a 37-star American flag, Iraq's Most Wanted playing cards, part of a camera found at ground zero in New York City, and a strand of George Washington's hair.

The museum didn't limit its history to displays. Fort Myers resident Mary Anne Passatore painted numerous murals on the walls, which further a visitor's experience by the depiction of scenes from various wars. The Civil War mural honors the Battle of Antietam, in which there were 24,000 casualties, states the mural. Passatore also painted the burning oil fields in Kuwait and the cold, deadly waters of Omaha Beach.

There are volunteer tour guides who will provide added information and make sure you don't overlook something interesting.

If You Go

Where: Southwest Florida Military Museum and Library, 4820 Leonard St., Cape Coral
More info:
www.veterans-foundation.org
or 239-541-8704

The museum offers a library, where there are comfortable couches, a computer, television and shelves filled with books. The museum also offers a good-sized gift shop. There, visitors can purchase T-shirts, jewelry, patches, ashtrays, hats, etc.

St. Petersburg Museum of History, St. Petersburg

Many baseball fans will watch the Rays at Tropicana Field in St. Petersburg. If you make the trip, stop in at the nearby St. Petersburg Museum of History for the Schrader's Little Cooperstown exhibit, which has the largest private collection of autographed baseballs in the world.

The exhibit displays more than 4,600 autographed baseballs.

It's a little dizzying to see all the balls on display, but the museum does a good job categorizing some of the autographs into themed areas such as Negro Leagues, Hall of Fame, or All-American Girls Professional League. There's a section on the museum's website that also allows you to find the location of your favorite player before you go to the museum.

For example, Andre Dawson is in L-12, Thurman Munson is in Q-1, and in the Yankees exhibit, Dale Murphy also is in two places, K-6 and L-6. To find your favorite players before you go to the museum, go here online: *www.spmoh.com/visit/exhibits/baseball/search/*.

Live Like A Tourist ... in Museums and Galleries

Where: St. Petersburg Museum of History, 335 Second Ave. NE, St. Petersburg
More info: 727-894-1052 and *www.spmoh.com*

The exhibit provides interesting information about the history of baseball, and especially spring training in Florida. For example, did you know the first team to train in St. Petersburg was the St. Louis Browns? Their first game was against the Cubs in front of more than 4,000 fans. Surprisingly, the Cubs won.

The Browns weren't the only team to train in St. Petersburg. Others include the Philadelphia Phillies, Boston Braves, New York Yankees, St. Louis Cardinals, New York Giants, New York Mets, Baltimore Orioles and Tampa Bay Rays. Interestingly, only six of the 30 major league teams have never held their spring training in the Sunshine State.

There's an exhibit about Joe DiMaggio and his marriage to Marilyn Monroe. On display is a ball she signed to him, "the greatest ballplayer," as well as a ball signed by both of them. It is believed to be one of only two balls in existence signed by the two American icons.

And, of course, there's a Rays exhibit. While the team's history isn't long, it's already storied — only in sports can a team drop the "Devil" from its name and start winning.

There's also a wall of balls signed by presidents, Olympians and celebrities, such as the Rolling Stones, Fats Domino and even Fidel Castro.

Baseball aside, the museum's largest exhibit is its history of the region.

There is a display detailing the styles of housing commonly used in the late 19th and early 20th centuries. ("More than 15 percent of the homes in St. Petersburg are classified as bungalows.") There are other displays detailing the history of the waterfront, the city's role in World War II and the original tribes living in Florida.

The St. Pete Museum of History also has a small exhibit showcasing artwork from the Florida Highwaymen as well as one called Century of Flight, highlighting the history of commercial airlines.

Tampa Bay History Center, Tampa

You can learn which four teams the Tampa Bay Lightning defeated on the way to winning the Stanley Cup, how many men manned a Seehund, and when Tampa's first cigar company opened.

These answers (New York Islanders, Montreal Canadiens, Philadelphia Flyers and Calgary Flames; two; and 1886) can be found at the Tampa Bay History Center, which is filled with fascinating exhibits.

The waterfront museum, which opened in 2009, takes visitors through the history of Florida, and specifically the Tampa Bay area. You'll find movies to watch, information to read, paintings to admire, and lots to learn about the history of this region.

The museum's permanent exhibits are quite interesting. Be sure to watch the "Winds of Change" film, which orients visitors to the state's history. Several

Live Like A Tourist ... **in Museums and Galleries**

exhibits provide the messy history of the natives and the Europeans, along with the Seminole Wars. The history of Tampa's cigar business also is interesting and includes a model of an old cigar factory, which was purposely built with large, open windows facing north and smaller ones on the south side to provide constant air flow. The models describe the functions performed on each level of the building. For example, "Tobacco was prepared on the uppermost floor, where moistened leaves were stripped of stems," the sign states. "The delicate fingers of women and children performed this task before child labor laws."

Visitors also can learn about the Port of Tampa, the city's history of sports, and much more.

After exploring the 60,000-square-foot museum, take a break and grab some food in the Columbia Cafe inside the Tampa Bay History Center, which is just as good as the original Ybor City restaurant. There also is a small gift shop attached to the museum.

The Florida Aquarium and Channelside are within walking distance (for those who are healthy), which can turn a half-day into a full day of fun in Tampa.

If You Go

What: Tampa Bay History Center, 801 Old Water St., Tampa
More info: *www.tampabayhistorycenter.org* or 813-228-0097

... With Animals

Big Cat Habitat, Sarasota

It's possible, even likely, that one day I'll live in a world where tigers no longer freely roam in the wild.

That's tragic.

The World Wildlife Fund estimates fewer than 3,200 tigers remain in the wild.

"Wild tiger numbers are at an all-time low," the WWF's website states. "We have lost 97 percent of wild tigers in just over a century."

Future generations might see tigers only in zoos and sanctuaries, such as the Big Cat Habitat and Gulf Coast Sanctuary in Sarasota.

Kay Rosaire began rescuing big cats, including tigers, in 1987. Kay's Big Cat Habitat became a nonprofit sanctuary in 2005, providing a home for animals and education to visitors.

The Big Cat Habitat isn't just a look-and-see kind of sanctuary. Kay and her staff offer education, hands-on activities, and a little entertainment as well.

"I was the youngest woman animal trainer in the world… and now I'm not," Kay said.

Visitors can expect to see and learn about bears, lions, ligers, tigers, primates, birds, llamas, tortoises and goats. Here are a few fun facts:
- Bengal tigers are considered to be excellent swimmers… which is strange, because my cat hates water. A tiger's lifespan is estimated between 10 and 15 years.
- Ligers exist. I thought a liger was a Napoleon Dynamite creation "bred for its skills in magic." So it turns out, a liger is real and can weigh more than 800 pounds.
- You cannot outrun a Kodiak brown bear, which, despite its large stature, can run up to 40 mph.

The bears are the first animals you'll likely notice upon entering the sanctuary, which houses Kodiak, Himalayan and Syrian bears. They seem to be full of personality, greeting visitors and playing in their swimming pools.

One of the more fun areas is the petting zoo, where visitors can mingle with tiny, little, adorable goats.

Live Like A Tourist … **with Animals**

The highlights for many, of course, are the big cats, all of which were born in captivity. The best viewing is from the aptly named catwalk, which provides guests with a closer look at the beautiful creatures.

If you go, make sure you are there for the educational demo led by Kay and/or her staff members. The show I observed included birds and tigers (not at the same time).

Kay narrated as the talented birds (macaws and cockatoos) roller-skated, put shapes in the matching holes, performed gymnastics skills on the rings, placed quarters into a piggy bank, and even rode a scooter.

As the birds entertained the crowd, Kay reminded everyone that some birds can live 70 to 100 years. And those who get one as a pet need to arrange for the bird's care. "Get a plan and a will," Kay advised.

"We highly recommend dogs and cats," Kay said. "They always have puppies and kittens at no-kill animal shelters. ... You'll have unconditional love."

Kay introduced the audience to two tigers. The first still had no name, as he only recently became a resident at the sanctuary. Kay works with the newbie to keep him occupied.

"It's better if their mind is busy," she said. "They stop fretting about past owners and think about the now."

Then she introduced longtime resident, Bambula, a female Bengal tiger. "She is one of my favorites," Kay said.

Kay explained that the sanctuary is about animal welfare, meaning they do their best to provide the "best possible quality of life."

"We don't believe in killing young, healthy animals," she said.

If You Go

Where: Big Cat Habitat and Gulf Coast Sanctuary, 7101 Palmer Blvd., Sarasota
More info: 941-371-6377, *BigCathabitat@yahoo.com* or *http://bigcathabitat.org/*

As Bambula made funny faces, jumped onto platforms and stood on top of a spinning globe, Kay reminded guests that Bambula's species faces extinction because of poachers. Never buy animal skins or body parts when visiting other countries, she urged. Those purchases support poachers, who will continue to kill tigers, rhinos and other endangered/threatened animals.

And it will be a very sad day when the beautifully, uniquely striped tigers exist only in zoos or sanctuaries... or worse, in history books.

For more about how to help protect endangered species, go to the World Wildlife Fund's website at *www.worldwildlife.org*.

Live Like A Tourist ... **with Animals**

The Butterfly Estates, Fort Myers

Butterflies flutter their paint-palette wings against a blue-sky canvas.

Like the watchful ocelli on a peacock's tail, the fashionable stripes of a zebra and the mesmerizing patterns of a mandarinfish (Google it), butterflies enhance our lives simply by their nature-made artwork.

Monarch butterflies, with their stained-glass-window wings, are gaining the attention of scientists and world leaders.

"East of the Rocky Mountains, the up to 1 billion monarchs that migrated to Mexico during the 1990s have declined to their lowest numbers in two decades," according to the National Wildlife Federation. "During the same period, western monarchs, which winter along the coast of California, have decreased by 90 percent. The primary culprit is habitat loss, particularly the elimination of nectar plants and milkweeds across millions of acres of agricultural land in the U.S. Midwest."

The White House invited 60 scientists, farmers and others to discuss the declining populations of pollinators, with a special focus on bees and monarch butterflies. A group of 50-plus researchers, educators and others wrote the president asking "to establish a multi-agency monarch butterfly recovery initiative to restore the habitats that support the extraordinary migrations of this iconic species," the letter states.

Live Like A Tourist ... **with Animals**

Locally, however, there is a group of dedicated people helping monarch butterflies, other butterflies and moths as well.

The Butterfly Estates in Fort Myers not only is breeding and raising butterflies native to Florida, but it also is educating visitors about planting butterfly gardens.

"We are an educational facility," said Mary Jane Wright, manager of the conservatory. "We are increasing our breeding program."

The Butterfly Estates houses a 3,600-square-foot glass conservatory filled with butterfly-friendly plants, where caterpillars can be seen on leaves and

If You Go

What: The Butterfly Estates, 1815 Fowler St., Fort Meyers
More info:
www.thebutterflyestates.com or 239-690-2359

limbs. Butterflies and moths air-dance above your head and onto flowers. It's a breathtaking, pulse-lowering experience.

"We consider it a real jewel right here in downtown Fort Myers," Mary Jane said.

There are signs educating visitors about mating habits, eyes, antennae (which is usually how you can tell a moth from a butterfly), and butterfly classifications. There are helpful employees on hand to answer questions as well. The conservatory sells plants, especially milkweed.

"We sell organic milkweed here," Mary Jane said. "We say: 'Plant milkweed. Plant milkweed.' ... (Monarchs) will only lay their eggs on milkweed."

In addition to the conservatory, visitors can do a little shopping (gifts, jewelry and decorations) and grab a bite (fudge, crepes, etc.). Sundays, there is a farmers market with a few vendors on-site.

This isn't an all-day attraction. If you are planning to bring little ones, you could pair it with the nearby Imaginarium Science Center, 2000 Cranford Ave., Fort Myers. If you are not bringing little ones, you also could work in a trip to the Southwest Florida Museum of History, 2031 Jackson St., Fort Myers; or to the Edison & Ford Winter Estates, 2350 McGregor Blvd., Fort Myers. The Butterfly Estates also can be contacted about playing host to princess birthday parties or other special events.

Clearwater Marine Aquarium, Clearwater

Many know the tale of Winter, the tail-less dolphin who triumphed despite her disability.

For those who don't know the story: Winter was found in December 2005 with her tail tightly wrapped in a crab trap line. She was only about 2 months old at the time.

"Winter was in critical condition and brought directly to Clearwater Marine Aquarium," states one of the many informational signs at the aquarium. "No one believed she would survive."

She wound up losing her tail along with a few vertebrae, making it impossible for her to swim in the normal up-and-down motion. Hanger Prosthetics learned about Winter, and made her a tail. A new mold is made at least once a year of Winter's peduncle so that she has a properly fitting prosthetic tail, which she wears one to three times a day during physical therapy.

Richard Ingber, president of Worldwide Marketing for Alcon Entertainment, also heard about Winter, and soon her tale was turned into a movie.

Winter now is a beautiful, happy dolphin living at Clearwater Marine Aquarium, where she has become famous since Warner Bros. released "Dolphin Tale," starring Morgan Freeman, Harry Connick Jr., Ashley Judd, Nathan Gamble and Kris Kristofferson. "Dolphin Tale 2" followed.

Clearwater Marine Aquarium isn't a quick trip (about two hours if you are in the Port Charlotte/Punta Gorda area), but it's worth it to see such an inspirational creature.

Live Like A Tourist ... with Animals

Winter helps you put your aches and pains into perspective. She's still swimming, whether she is wearing her prosthetic or not. She perseveres.

While Winter's tale is moving, I found myself even more inspired by the humans caring for her. I wanted to hug Cammie Zodrow, the senior marine mammal trainer, as she affectionately worked with Winter in the water. The trainers could have their own documentary/reality show/Hollywood treatment. They are a selfless group of humans, dedicating their careers to caring for creatures who otherwise would be dead. We often praise nurses, doctors, teachers, firefighters, police (as we should), but we often forget about the animal caregivers. We do so much harm to animals in the wild that it's truly heart-warming to see the trainers, like Cammie, working with Winter.

Training time varies throughout the day with Winter, so be sure to listen to the announcements broadcast throughout the aquarium. There are many other daily presentations such as "River Otters," "Stingray Feeding," "Guess that Pelican," "Sea Turtle Nesting" or "Meet our Turtles." Guests will be provided with a sheet containing the day's presentations.

If You Go

Where: Clearwater Marine Aquarium, 249 Windward Passage, Clearwater

Tips: About half of it is outdoors, so dress for it. A trolley or boat will take you back and forth to both attractions. If you have difficulty walking, take the trolley for door-to-door service.

More info: 727-441-1790 or *www.seewinter.com*

The aquarium is separated into two facilities. There's the aquarium part, where Winter lives along with her dolphin buddy, Hope, who was discovered as a calf in distress in December 2010. She was found with her deceased mother, still trying to nurse. Hope is featured in "Dolphin Tale 2." Visitors to the aquarium also will see otters, sea turtles, stingrays and two nurse sharks named Thelma and Louise.

The second facility is the Winter's Dolphin Tale Adventure, which is all air-conditioned and a good place to cool off after being at the aquarium. This is where visitors can learn about the film, see props from the set and watch clips from the film.

A free trolley or boat ride is offered between the two facilities.

There is a large gift shop at both locations, where there are adorable T-shirts, stuffed animals, jewelry and other souvenirs. There also are places to grab quick lunches or snacks as well.

Live Like A Tourist ... **with Animals**

Everglades Wonder Gardens, Bonita Springs

Before Cinderella's castle opened, before Lebron took his talents to South Beach, and before sunburned bodies zipped down water slides, Florida offered different forms of entertainment for tourists.

Quirky roadside attractions lured travelers off U.S. 41. These places gave motorists a chance to stretch their legs, grab a bite to eat and experience sometimes strange things they wouldn't normally see in Iowa, Ohio, Massachusetts, etc.

Because a lot of families prefer spending vacations in amusement parks, large cities, or at sporting events, many of these roadside attractions have gone the way of station wagon road trips.

Southwest Florida, which retains so much of the state's original charm, still houses a few of these roadside attractions.

Everglades Wonder Gardens, in Bonita Springs, first opened in 1936. I have no idea what it was like back then, but I can imagine as a Midwesterner that in a pre-Internet, pre-cable TV world, the Everglades Wonder Gardens seemed as exotic as an issue of National Geographic.

"The attraction has been a focal point of Bonita Springs since Bill and Lester Piper created the facility to rehabilitate injured animals," states the website. "The park has remained in the Piper family ever since and has become a place for visitors to enjoy the botanical jungle and see Florida's wildlife in an intimate way, something that modern parks cannot provide."

As the decades passed, tourist attractions became like Major League Baseball players… some grew a little too big, too fast. Southwest Florida didn't grow in steroidal ways, and therefore managed to hold on to places like Everglades Wonder Gardens or the Shell Factory in North Fort Myers.

But in 2013, Everglades Wonder Gardens did close for a short time.

"I strictly took it over so it wouldn't go away," said John Brady, a local photographer who is leasing the gardens. He has formed a nonprofit and hopes to eventually buy it. "There was an opportunity to preserve it and that's what we've been doing so far."

Everglades Wonder Gardens is a wonderful place to take young children, northern friends, or tropical plant lovers. The best way to tour the gardens is to loop it, which John usually tells guests as they enter the attraction. But it's not a large facility so you won't miss anything if you venture clockwise, counter-clockwise or skip around in a random pattern.

If You Go

Where: Everglades Wonder Gardens, 27180 Old U.S. 41, Bonita Springs
More info: 239-992-2591, *http://evergladeswondergardens.com*

Here are the must-see attractions:

First, the alligators. I've been living in Florida now for more than a decade, and I've yet to tire of seeing or photographing alligators. Perhaps it's the element of danger. Perhaps it's their size. Perhaps it's their strength. Perhaps it's the hope there will be a new football coach soon… oops, wrong Gators.

Back to my point before I make a crab legs joke to balance out the UF-FSU rivalry… there are two-dozen-plus alligators swimming and sunning themselves at Everglades Wonder Gardens. And they do this within a few feet of you, separated only by fencing.

But the coolest/scariest/most thrilling part of it all: You can walk across a low-hanging, swinging bridge above the swimming hole where the alligators are clearly looking at you as a possible meal if an earthquake/tornado/sinkhole/random missile strike suddenly wipes out the bridge. It's awesomely terrifying for a Midwestern native.

The second must-see area is the Flamingo Pond/Park. Though Florida has amazing birds (sandhill cranes, herons, osprey, etc.), flamingos are a fun group/gaggle to observe.

The third area is really more of an overall observation. The gardens are filled with bromeliads, orchids and other beautiful tropical plants. There are designated areas with informational markers, so keep an eye out to learn more about the trees and plants.

The fourth area, and this might be the weirdest one for me, is the strange relationship I developed with a green iguana who for some reason couldn't stop staring at me. Then, he started smiling… or so I suspected. And then, he smashed his mouth into the glass directly in front of me. I have no idea why. I have no idea why I found this amusing. But this is a prime example of why roadside attractions are such unique places which should continue to exist in Florida.

Kudos to John Brady for his enthusiasm and passion. Also, spend some time looking at his amazing photography, which is for sale in the gift shop/museum area of Everglades Wonder Gardens. If you are shopping nearby at Coconut Point or in Estero, take a few hours out of your day and enjoy a good old-fashioned, Florida roadside attraction.

Live Like A Tourist … with Animals

Florida Aquarium, Tampa

Some can fearlessly snorkel or dive alongside eels, sharks, stingrays and other large toothy-barbed-stinging critters.

I'm not one of those people.

I'd be cool hanging out with Nemo, Dory, Sebastian and even Don Ira Feinberg (not related), but there are no sea prisons to house the scary, mean creatures. That's why I enjoy visiting aquariums.

Florida Aquarium in Tampa is an awesome environment for nervous Nellies to get an up-close look at eels, sharks, stingrays, jellyfish and even Burmese pythons. It also educates visitors about our environment here in Florida, and others around the globe.

The large aquarium opened near Channelside Bay Plaza in 1995, generating a $60 million impact to the Tampa Bay community in its first year, according to Florida Aquarium's website.

The beautiful, waterfront aquarium since has added several exhibits and features.

The Wetlands Trail exhibit takes visitors deep into a Florida river, where an alligator's mesmerizing eyeballs can be viewed safely behind glass. We see gators all the time, but it really is a remarkable creature to admire up close.

Across the aisle are more fun critters to watch: the ever-popular river otters who constantly swim and dive with the boundless energy of a caffeine-charged toddler. Because of its enviable metabolic rate, river otters usually eat between 15 and 20 percent of their body weight each day, according to Florida State University.

There also are several species of birds in The Wetlands Trail exhibit, including the quirky roseate spoonbill. The pink-feathered bird with the funny beak was nearly hunted to extinction. Conservation efforts have helped the birds rebound, but they remain a Species of Special Concern in Florida and

Live Like A Tourist ... **with Animals**

in Louisiana, according to the National Audubon Society. There are only an estimated 30,750 roseate spoonbills in North America.

"The Florida Wetlands Trail dome's architectural design is comprised of 1,100 glass panels and mimics the outer spirals of a nautilus shell, a theme continued inside the aquarium as guests follow a continuing spiral back to the first floor of the lobby and touch tank," states the website.

Journey to Madagascar is another fascinating area, where visitors can watch the endangered ring-tailed lemurs play. Guests also can walk into a small, freaky exhibit where you can see and hear hissing cockroaches. In case you were wondering, the Madagascar cockroaches make that hissing sound by exhaling air through breathing holes, according to National Geographic.

The Coral Reef is a must-visit exhibit as well. "The coral reef gallery simulates a 60-foot dive starting in shallow-water reefs and descending to deeper waters. Each viewing window presents a micro habitat which changes as the depth increases," states the website. "The coral reef exhibit is modeled after the coral formations of the Dry Tortugas off the Florida Keys. Housed in a 500,000-gallon tank, the coral reef provides the base for this vibrant community of more than 2,000 coral reef residents, representing 100 species, many native to Florida."

This is where a guest could sit for hours, mesmerized by the stealthy sand tiger sharks and all the other sea life around them. This is where you may see the puppet-like green moray eels, friendly stingrays and Disney-cute reef fish.

Those looking for more adventure can take advantage of the aquarium's Dive with the Sharks program, which allows certified-SCUBA divers a chance to swim with the mighty beasts. Those who are not certified SCUBA divers can participate in the Swim with the Fishes program. More information on both opportunities is available online: *www.flaquarium.org.*

A trip to the aquarium could take an entire day, or a few hours. It all depends on your speed, your children's tolerance levels, etc.

The aquarium offers some food at the Café Ray, which is open daily. If you choose this route, I recommend getting a snack and then grabbing dinner at one of Channelside's many restaurants. The Caribbean Cantina, which is a full-service restaurant, is open "Saturdays and Sundays in the Fall/Winter and daily during peak seasons (call to confirm days)," states the website.

Before you leave, the aquarium has a gift shop — a perfect place to get souvenirs or holiday gifts.

If You Go

Where: The Florida Aquarium, 701 Channelside Drive, Tampa

More info: 813-273-4000 or *www.flaquarium.org*

Live Like A Tourist ... **with Animals**

Mote Marine Laboratory and Aquarium, Sarasota

I found Nemo.

I also found Dory and a lot of their friends at the Mote Marine Laboratory and Aquarium in Sarasota.

The aquarium is a fantastic place to take little ones, or big ones for that matter. Round ones, square ones, long ones, short ones, young ones and old ones all can enjoy it too. It's really a place for everyone.

Mote, which began as a small science lab, has evolved into a large complex in Sarasota with offices and stations located throughout the state.

"It's gotten pretty big," said Hayley Rutger, public relations coordinator.

Mote, which employs nearly 200 and uses almost 1,600 volunteers, has scientists working outside the state as well.

"We work all over the world," Rutger said. "We have scientists working in Israel and in Japan. We have worked on six of seven continents."

Some of their work is visible at the aquarium, where visitors can frequent 365 days a year.

Mote is working on growing coral to replace the reefs that are dying due to ocean acidification (sometimes called osteoporosis of the sea), water pollution and temperature change.

Mote raises sturgeon and harvests caviar, which it then sells in Whole Foods Market.

The most brilliant species also is bred at Mote: seahorses. Why are seahorses so special and smart? The females let the males give birth...

Live Like A Tourist ... with Animals

about every 28 days. OK, so maybe the females don't "let" the males, but it's interesting nonetheless.

Most of the sea life displayed in the aquarium is local, or at least found in parts of Florida.

"We try to show off Florida species," she said.

My favorite exhibit at Mote happens to belong to two of the biggest Florida critters: Hugh and Buffett, manatees born at the Miami Seaquarium.

Both have lived at Mote since 1996. There's a good chance you'll see them eating because that's what they seem to do all day. They eat 72 to 96 heads of romaine lettuce and kale each day. They also eat carrots, beets, apples and monkey biscuits with vitamins.

The aquarium isn't a look-only place. It's very interactive, making it a fun place for kids.

There's the Contact Cove, where visitors can touch a five-toothed sea cucumber, a pencil urchin or a flat claw hermit crab. There's also the Ray Touch Pool where kids can touch stingrays.

At Fossil Creek, guests can purchase a bucket of sand and sift through looking for fossils and sharks teeth.

Hanging above the entrance to the shark training pool is the Great Hammerhead caught by Bucky Dennis in May 2006 near Boca Grande. It was unique because she weighed 1,280 pounds and she was carrying 56 pups.

Be sure to check out the large gift shop before leaving. There are adorable, one-of-a-kind gifts you can't find elsewhere.

Mote offers a cute diner, but I had to check out The Old Salty Dog.

There are two locations in Sarasota, and I had never been to the one directly across the street from Mote, which was featured on the television show "Man v. Food." Of course, I had to order the famous Salty Dog, which is described as a "quarter-pound hot dog dipped in our batter and fried to a golden brown," on its website. It was served with fries, cole slaw or veggies (though you might as well just pile on the fries when you're ordering a fried hot dog).

The restaurant is located right on the water. Boaters and kayakers can pull right up to the dock. Dogs are welcome, but it might be weird serving a Salty Dog to a dog at the Old Salty Dog.

Naples Zoo at Caribbean Gardens, Naples

"The honey badger don't care…"

If you know that reference, you've likely laughed at Randall's honey badger video on YouTube. Warning: It's not a kid-friendly video.

The video sparked interest in honey badgers, which are known as one of the fiercest animals. (It has been documented on camera challenging a cobra.) And the only place to see honey badgers in the Southeastern United States is at the Naples Zoo at Caribbean Gardens.

The Naples Zoo is one of four accredited zoos in the country to house the frightening yet strangely cuddly-looking honey badgers. The honey badger is one of many interesting exhibits at the Naples Zoo, which first began 95 years ago as Dr. Henry Nehrling's botanical gardens.

The history of the gardens is as fascinating as the zoo itself. But here's a short version:

Nehrling, who believed in conservation, wrote in 1904: "It is high time to protect and preserve what is still left in Florida."

At one point, he had about 3,000 tropical plants that attracted scientists and inventors (including Thomas Edison) from around the country.

"In later years, the site lost many of its plants when Nehrling became a victim of swindlers. And following his death in 1929, locals raided his nursery and removed rare plants that could be transplanted," states the website.

Julius Fleischmann eventually took over the land, and began converting what was left of Nehrling's trees into botanical gardens.

"Fleischmann created a tropical showplace for his guests to enjoy," states the website. "By 1954, complete with an array of

Live Like A Tourist … **with Animals**

tropical birds, the garden was ready to delight guests once again and now under the name Caribbean Gardens."

In 1967, zoo operators Larry and Nancy Jane Tezlaff visited the gardens. After Fleischmann's death, the Tezlaffs were asked if they were interested in bringing animals to the gardens. The Tezlaffs, known as Jungle Larry and Safari Jane, then opened in 1969.

In 2002, the Fleischmann family announced their interest in selling the "43 acres of zoo property and the nearly 120 surrounding acres," states the website. The community responded, and overwhelmingly approved a referendum allowing the county to purchase the land… and thus save the zoo… and the honey badgers.

There are several shows throughout the day at various locations around the zoo. For example, you can attend a "Meet the Keeper" show at one of the animal exhibits such as honey badgers, cheetahs, giraffes, etc. And speaking of giraffes, visitors can feed giraffes for a fee.

There are two other can't-miss shows including the Feature Show in the Safari Canyon Open-Air Theater. There, the witty and intelligent zoo employees provide interesting information while showcasing animals such as Belize, the ocelot; Molly, the sloth; or Knox, the barn owl. In case you were wondering, a barn owl can eat about eight mice a day.

The other can't-miss show: Alligator Bay Feeding.

Obviously, alligator feeding is illegal for people like you and me. But at the zoo, reptile keepers like Mark Mullen, can educate visitors while getting a good look at the alligators who respond to their names during the daily program.

In addition, expect to see leopards, zebras, snakes (eeks), black bears and primates.

Expect to spend at least a half-day at the zoo. If you are someone who reads informational signs and enjoys entertaining shows, carve out a full day.

And don't forget to look at the beautiful, tropical flowers and trees in addition to the giraffes and the honey badgers. After all, the land once was a garden… even though "the honey badger don't care."

If You Go

Where: Naples Zoo at Caribbean Gardens, 1590 Goodlette-Frank Road, Naples
More info: 239-262-5409 or *www.napleszoo.org*
Tips: If you plan to bring a stroller, and if you have a choice of strollers, bring the one more geared for off-roading. Most of the trails are paved, but some paths are gravel/rocky. Also, wear sunscreen and comfortable shoes.

Octagon Wilderness Sanctuary, Punta Gorda

Squiggy is a 17-year-old grizzly bear who was beaten with pipes. His 13-year-old Himalayan brown bear sisters, Laverne and Shirley, also were rescued from the same group that tried training Squiggy for commercials.

The three now live happily in a home in eastern Charlotte County. They even have their own pool.

Squiggy, Laverne and Shirley are among 200 animals living at the Octagon Wilderness Sanctuary, which is kind of like a retirement home for abused, abandoned, rescued or unwanted exotic animals.

While it's open to the public, don't go in thinking it's a zoo with cotton candy and trams. Octagon actually provides closer access to the animals while still abiding by state and federal regulations. It's a more intimate setting.

The animals come from other rescue groups, zoos, circuses, private owners, etc. They may have been abused like Squiggy. They may have been owned by idiots who thought a tiger would make a good pet or bodyguard. They are exotic animals who through no fault of their own lived tough lives before entering Octagon.

Live Like A Tourist ... **with Animals**

"We get them from all over the country," said volunteer Roger Dickinson.

Roger and his wife, Jane, have volunteered at Octagon for about five years. The Connecticut natives have no biology/zoology backgrounds — just a love for animals, including their own at home: Bingo the golden retriever, Sweet Pea the canary, and Jule the fish.

"We love animals," Roger said.

Roger and Jane, of Punta Gorda, are among a small army of volunteers that keeps Octagon up and running.

"It's 100 percent volunteer and 100 percent donations," Roger said.

Roger and Jane volunteer on Wednesdays, and sometimes on Saturdays.

"On Wednesdays, we do a lot of cleaning and then we feed the bears," he said. "The big cats eat at night."

If You Go

Where: Octagon Wildlife Sanctuary, 41660 Horseshoe Road, Punta Gorda (off State Road 31)
More info: 239-543-1130 or *www.octagonwildlife.com*

Typical volunteer duties can include filling water dishes, cleaning habitats/enclosures, separating and preparing food, feeding animals, landscaping, general maintenance, according to the website.

Jane entered the enclosure belonging to one of Octagon's newest residents, Beamer the sloth. Of course, the sloth did just what you'd expect a sloth would do — nothing. He stayed curled up in a ball sleeping next to a stuffed animal.

Baloo, a Himalayan black bear, loves Roger. In fact, he loves most people. Baloo previously worked for the Moscow Circus. The informational sign about him states that he "seems to love people and sweets, but not other bears." Thus, Baloo has his own pool suite.

"Every tiger has a pool and every bear has a pool," Roger said.

Two parrots named Rainbow and Harley also call Octagon home, but they more likely call it their (expletive) home. Apparently, they once lived in a dentist's office before someone taught them every curse word invented at the time. I met Rainbow and Harley, and they must have been in good moods because they greeted me with a normal hello, followed by no other choice words.

In addition to tigers, bears and cursing parrots, visitors can see Tumble, a black and white ruffled lemur; Hector, a binturong, or bear cat; Lilly, a black leopard; and many others.

Live Like A Tourist ... **with Animals**

. . . While Exploring

Antiquing in Arcadia

West Oak Street may just be one of the priciest stretches of real estate in Southwest Florida — if you include the treasures inside the dozen-plus antique stores.

You literally can find anything on West Oak Street.

In addition to the typical glassware, china, crystal, salt-and-pepper shakers, etc., one shopping trip included finds such as a Red Dog beer tapper handle, a 4-foot R2-D2 drink cooler, a Cheer Bear cookie jar, a Nazi flag (actually more than one), an orange O.J. Simpson football, an accordion and a coffin.

Yes, a coffin. It's listed as an "early 20th century coffin with single plank lid — a rare find."

I'd say.

The cost: $450. It didn't indicate if it had ever been used.

Thousands of people visit this small stretch of West Oak Street each year for antiquing.

Visitors should dedicate an entire day to antiquing in Arcadia. There are simply too many stores — some of which are quite large and "filled to the rim with Brim" (which, if referring to the 1980s coffee commercial, Brim would not be considered an antique yet).

Frankly, it's hard to find an exact definition of an antique. Some say 50 years. Some say 100. As a nonprofessional antiquer (Is that a word?), I guess it's safe to say that anything at least 100 years old is an antique. Anything younger may be considered vintage or a collectible. (Kids, do not refer to your parents or grandparents as vintage... not a good idea.)

Whether it's 50 years or 100, one of the more interesting finds in several stores were the Florida Highwaymen paintings.

Live Like A Tourist ... **While Exploring**

The Florida Highwaymen are described as a "group of 26 African-American self-taught artists that started painting in the 1950s and were successful in their painting careers in the 1960s and 1970s," according to floridahighwaymen.com.

The paintings originally sold for $25 or $35, according to the website.

Some sell today for more than $1,000.

The Highwaymen painted the vibrant Florida landscapes quickly and are believed to have sold more than 150,000 paintings.

According to a 2012 NPR article, some famous collectors include former Gov. Jeb Bush, first lady Michelle Obama and director Steven Spielberg.

In addition to the Highwaymen paintings, those looking for military collectibles and antiques can find uniforms, patches, coins, etc., in various stores along West Oak Street.

Whether it's paintings, books, records (kids, ask someone older than 30 what these are), wagon wheels or jewelry, there's something for everyone in Arcadia.

If You Go

Where: Arcadia, FL
More info:
www.arcadiaflantiques.com

While exploring the shelves and walls for antiques, be sure to take note of the buildings as well. The creaking wood floors in some stores may remind visitors of their parents' or grandparents' homes, when their little feet tried unsuccessfully to replicate the groans of the aging wood. Same with the way the air conditioning slowly dissipates the farther one enters some stores... just like the way grandma's kitchen air seemed more lived-in than perhaps the cooler living/parlor room.

A full day of antiquing and nostalgia requires a break for lunch.

Check out Mary Margaret's Tea and Biscuit, 10 S. Polk Ave., in the Arcade Building. I greatly enjoyed the lobster bisque and chicken salad on a croissant served with fresh fruit. I'm not a tea person, but I've heard their tea is fabulous. If this doesn't strike your fancy, there are plenty of other places to grab a bite to eat or a drink within walking distance.

ECHO Global Farms, North Fort Myers

Clear Gulf of Mexico waters where the fish flop, dolphins leap and people play. Amusement parks where friendly characters greet wide-eyed dreamers. Lush, green golf courses where the great game entices golfers, regardless of skills.

These are the typical tourism images for Florida.

Then there's this:

A 50-acre site where some of the brightest young minds are working hard to make the world a better place. Sounds like a cliché, right? It's not. It's life at ECHO International Headquarters in North Fort Myers.

In a nutshell: "Approximately 925 million people in the world are hungry… Our purpose is to help those who are teaching farmers around the world know how to be more effective in producing enough to meet the needs of their families and their communities. They, in turn, teach others, and the ECHO effect continues," ECHO's website states.

Fifteen acres of this Lee County campus is designated for the Global Farms, where tours are provided several times a week.

The Global Farm is where eight interns work to develop better farming techniques that can be shared in developing countries and in urban communities.

Here are a few facts you may learn from your intern/tour guide, or from informational signs throughout the farm:

- A typical small farmer raises only half the amount of food needed to feed his family.
- African, Asian and South American farms lose soil "at twice the rate that is sustainable for crop production."
- Twelve plants and five animal species produce 75 percent of the world's food.

The interns (who spend a year living and working at ECHO) are assigned to one of these areas of the Global Farm: Lowlands,

Live Like A Tourist … **While Exploring**

Urban, Monsoon, Mountain, Appropriate Technologies, Rainforest, Semi-Arid and Community Garden.

Much of the interns' food comes from the very farm they maintain. The interns also care for animals such as chickens, goats, tilapia and ducks.

These are just a few examples of what these interns were studying and accomplishing:

- In the Lowlands region (which is similar to Vietnam, Thailand and the Philippines): They were working on the SRI (System for Rice Intensification), which may result in healthier, bigger crops that use less water and seedlings.
- In the Urban area (where there's little soil or space): They were working on growing fruits and vegetables on roofs, alongside buildings and on carpets (believe it or not, and it's called Wick Gardens).
- In the Semi-Arid region (which may include areas of Central India, near the Sahara Desert in Africa, and the West Coast of South America): Interns were testing soils. All of the plants in the experiment area were treated with Lee County compost and partially composted goat manure. Half, separated by a line, "also had mixed into the holes a small amount of charred rice hulls (biochar) that had been inoculated with effective microorganisms. The hope was to boost the nutrient profile and beneficial microbial activity in the holes with the biochar."

Success at Southwest Florida's ECHO can be seen around the world. The moringa plant, which is high in vitamins and grows on the North Fort Myers farm, now is being grown successfully in schoolyards and gardens in Laos, according to ECHO.

ECHO operates Regional Impact Centers in Chiang Mai, Thailand; Arusha, Tanzania; and Ouagadougou, Burkina Faso. ECHO also is conducting a long-term research project in soil science based near Modimolle, South Africa, according to its website.

If You Go

Where: ECHO International Headquarters, 17391 Durrance Road, North Fort Myers
Tips: Wear comfortable shoes.
More info: 239-543-3246, *info@echonet.org* or *http://echonet.org*

At the North Fort Myers headquarters, there is a research library, a seed bank and staff offices. There also is a nursery and a gift shop, where seeds, T-shirts, books and other souvenirs can be purchased.

Ellenton Ice and Sports Complex

There's one sure way to cool off: ice skating.

Judy Jones, of Bradenton, brought her grandson, Michael Gentry, to the Ellenton Ice and Sports Complex in Manatee County. She usually brings Michael to the rink a few times a year when he visits from Virginia.

"This is a wonderful rink," Judy said, as the energetic Michael quickly skated laps around others during public skating hours at the complex. The public skating hours vary, so be sure to check the website.

There are a few guidelines for the public skating hours: "No jumps, no sit spin and camel spin on the ice," the website states. Trust me, I won't be jumping on skates. I also have no idea what a camel spin is, and if I ever did one, it would have been an accident and looked more like a squid spin.

While amateurs and young hockey players, like Michael, skate laps in one rink, young Olympic hopefuls are skating, leaping and probably camel spinning in another rink. That's what makes the Ellenton Ice Complex so interesting — even if you aren't skating. Being able to watch young pairs skaters like Jonah Barrett, of Celebration, Fla., and Elli Kopmar, of Seattle, is a special sight.

Three Ellenton-based pairs skaters earned their way to the Winter Olympics in Sochi: Felicia Zhang and Nate Bartholomay, Stacey Kemp and David King, and Paige Lawrence and Rudi Swiegers.

Anyone interested in learning to skate can do so from some of the top coaches in the country. The following are just some of the experienced coaches at Ellenton:

- Skating School Director Lyndon Johnston is a two-time Olympian, 1989 World Silver Pair Medalist, and Canadian National Single and Pairs Champion. In 1993, he was inducted into the Manitoba Sports Hall of Fame and Museum.

Live Like A Tourist ... **While Exploring**

- Coach Jim Peterson is a World and Olympic coach and choreographer, 2009 Professional Skaters Association and U.S. Olympic Committee Developmental Coach of the Year, and 2010 Professional Skaters Association Developmental Coach of the Year.
- Amanda Evora is a 2010 Olympic competitor, two-time World competitor, and five-time U.S. Championships Pair Medalist.

Eight-week beginner skating lessons are offered throughout the year for both kids and adults. And for those who can skate, there are youth and adult hockey leagues.

For those who squid spin on skates, the complex includes an indoor turf area, where soccer, field hockey and lacrosse can be played. The field can be rented for leagues or parties, and there are open soccer hours. Again, check the online schedule for available hours.

The Ellenton Ice and Sports Complex has a fitness center, as well as classes such as yoga and kung-fu. It seems like a long way to drive for a gym workout, but it could work out well for parents who have children taking lessons.

If You Go

What: Ellenton Ice and Sports Complex
Where: 5309 29th St. E, Ellenton (off Interstate 75, Exit 224)
When: Hours vary for public skating. Check the website, *http://ellentonice.com/publicskating.*
More info: 941-723-3663 or *http://ellentonice.com*

And for those who just don't like physical activities, there are some video games scattered around the complex.

After a day of skating or playing soccer, head over the nearby Ellenton Premium Outlets mall. There, shoppers can find bargains at clothing stores such as Columbia, J. Crew, Banana Republic, etc. There also are high-end stores such as Coach and Dooney & Bourke. Athletes can find plenty of deals at Adidas, Reebok, Under Armour, Nike and Puma, among others.

Members of the military, veterans and their families can show their IDs to receive a VIP coupon book at the information center. And on Tuesdays, those who are at least 50 years old can receive a 10 percent discount at certain stores. Check at the information center for the most updated list of participating stores.

Fishermen's Village, Punta Gorda

Remember your first year living in Southwest Florida?

Where did you take visitors? Where did you buy birthday and Christmas gifts?

Fishermen's Village in Punta Gorda, right?

It is *the* place in Charlotte County to enjoy local, unique shopping, waterfront dining and cruises. It can be a destination for lunch, or an entire vacation as Fishermen's Village also offers villas.

It attracts an estimated 1.5 million visitors a year and received the TripAdvisor Certificate of Excellence with reviewers giving it four out of five stars.

"This is our first stop with visitors. Wonderful variety of shops and restaurants, entertainment and special events," wrote one visitor on TripAdvisor. "Don't forget there are boat rides available to visit the barrier islands or to spend the day fishing. You will find a marina and overnight accommodations as well as a Realtor or even get a haircut. You cannot beat the opulent Christmas light display from the entrance to the waterway at Fishermen's Village. Definitely the best in the area!"

The roots of Fishermen's Village date back to the 1920s.

"Fishermen's Village stands on the site of the Maud Street City Docks, which were built in 1928-29 to replace the old King Street pier," according to "Fishtales, the Story of Fishermen's Village." "The King Street pier was home to the fish packing houses, or plants, that were integral to the fishing industry of the area."

By the mid-1930s, Punta Gorda Fish Company and the West Coast Fish Company were the only two plants operating there at the time.

"The pier was also occupied by the Gulf Oil Co. which had a bulk storage facility located where the current Village Oyster Bar was established. Across from this was Matt Week's Boat Shop, which had adjoining shore space for boat sheds and marine ways. This area is now occupied by the tennis courts and parking lots," according to "Fishtales."

"In 1939, a fire destroyed the two large packing plants. The West Coast Fish Co. folded but the Punta Gorda Fish Co. continued to operate on a much smaller scale. ... The dock and remaining buildings fell into disrepair. In 1977, the city council felt this

Live Like A Tourist ... **While Exploring**

property could be better utilized. In 1980, Fishermen's Village was constructed as an integral part of a historic community boasting waterfront shopping, dining, a resort and marina featuring boutiques, fishing charters, Charlotte Harbor boating excursions, boat and kayak rentals, villa vacation rentals, salon and spa, Military Heritage Museum, live entertainment and special events."

Stephanie and Filip Sahm have owned the Caribongo for 10 years. Their popular store offers shirts, jewelry, nail polish and other items that change colors in the sun. "I love it," Stephanie said of Fishermen's Village. "It's the best. It's the best place to work. Best customers."

Bob and Joann Filkins, of Punta Gorda, regularly visit Fishermen's Village. It's become part of their weekly routine, and their health routine as they walk trails in the area and end up at The Good Ole' Days Coffee and Ice Cream shop for iced coffee. "We come at least four times a week," Joann said.

On Tuesdays, a group of their friends gather there for what they call their Coffee Clan meetings. "We love it," she said.

If You Go

Where: Fishermen's Village, 1200 W. Retta Esplanade, Punta Gorda
More info: 941-639-8721 or *www.fishville.com*
Tips: Take money. It will be hard to walk away empty-handed.

The stores offer a variety of goods: soaps, raincoats for dogs, "Walking Dead" Monopoly, stained glass decorations, shoes, Punta Gorda attire, homemade fudge, etc.

There currently are three restaurants: Village Fish Market, The Captain's Table and Harpoon Harry's. A fourth restaurant, Scotty's Brewhouse, is expected to open as part of a two-phase, $40 million renovation. Other phase one renovations include a new main entrance, additional parking, center court improvements, Harborwalk extension and improved restrooms.

Phase two, which is expected to take about five years to complete, includes:
- A new mixed-use building that will house restaurants, shops and a new marina facility.
- A parking deck for about 150 additional parking spaces.
- And, an impressive "sand beach with zero-entry and negative edge pool, overlooking the harbor," according to Fishermen's Village.

In the meantime, enjoy the shops and restaurants. Also, consider taking a cruise or fishing charter.

For more information on all that Fishermen's Village offers, go to *www.fishville.com*.

Live Like A Tourist ... **While Exploring**

Fleamasters Fleamarket, Fort Myers

Sometimes you need a monkey to hold your bottle of wine.

Other times, you just need a leather belt, a piece of luggage or a new rug to replace that old one in the living room.

Fleamasters Fleamarket in Fort Myers can fulfill any of those needs, and many more, with its 900 stores and 400,000 square feet of retail space.

Walter Kuechle operates one of the most interesting stores in Fleamasters Fleamarket, which is open only from 9 a.m. to 5 p.m. Fridays, Saturdays and Sundays. The hours may shorten out of season.

It's hard not to smile in Walter's store, G & W's Depot. The name doesn't indicate it, but Walter's store is filled with fun. You'll find board games and card games, magic sets, chess sets, bingo supplies, dominoes, puzzles, yo-yos and more.

"It just keeps getting bigger and bigger," he said. "I got a lot of stuff."

Fellow business owners and shoppers stop by regularly, even during these slower summer months. It seems everyone knows Walter, who has been selling toys and making people happy for 26 years now at Fleamasters Fleamarket.

"Hi, Walter," greet passersby.

"I love people and they love me," Walter said.

Shoppers can find a variety of themed Monopoly board games such as Jerseyopoly, My Little Pony, National Parks, New York City, Christmas, etc. Fans of the game Trivial Pursuit also can find specialty versions about the Rolling Stones, the Beatles or Classic Rock (which came home with me).

Live Like A Tourist ... **While Exploring**

Walter keeps up with the trends, and makes sure he has popular games for families and adults in stock. Sequence has been a popular one lately, as has the cleverly designed game, The Game of Baloney.

"I got so many games, you can't even count," he said.

If fun isn't your game, perhaps you prefer a different sport of sorts.

Stanley Kaniuka, co-owner of Sports n Stuff, has been in business for five years at Fleamasters.

The Chicago native sells sports-themed attire, such as clothes, decorations and flags. And don't worry, he sells more than Bulls, Bears and Blackhawks goods.

And if sports and games aren't what you are looking for, fear not. There's everything and anything for sale: souvenirs, shells, bedding, skin-care products, makeup, candles, figurines, decorations, sunglasses, jewelry, pet supplies, shoes, antiques, and even T-shirts that reveal colored images in the sunshine.

If You Go

Where: Fleamasters Fleamarket, 4135 Dr. Martin Luther King Jr. Blvd. (close to Interstate 75), Fort Myers

Tips: Wear comfortable walking shoes and dress for the heat (although there are fans, misters and some air-conditioned areas)

More info: 239-334-7001 or *www.fleamall.com*

Truthfully, I was worried about shopping at Fleamasters Fleamarket in July. I worried it might be uncomfortably hot. It's not. There are fans in every hallway, and some of them spray mist as well. Some stores also are air-conditioned.

All the shopping and walking may result in an appetite, or at least a thirst.

Stanley recommends the pizza, salads and hot dogs, which are served in small food court areas. There's also places offering barbecue, pretzels, ice cream and even beer.

If you are looking for something fresher to take home, there are several produce stands in and around the flea market where you can purchase ripe strawberries, cucumbers, peppers, etc.

I would strongly suggest getting a copy of the Market Guide upon entry, as it has a map and a store locater inside the magazine. If you are like me, with a missing inner compass, you will need the map, as Fleamasters Fleamarket is quite large. Some of the ads in the Market Guide are coupons or offer discounts if you mention the ad, so be sure to flip through it before you start shopping at the market where you can find just about anything... including that wine-holding monkey.

Laishley Park, Punta Gorda

Not too long ago, if you wandered into Laishley Park, you were either fishing or lost.

You weren't going there to eat sushi.

You weren't going to buy art.

You weren't going to let your kids dance and skip beneath cool squirts of water.

And you certainly weren't going to the No. 1 ice cream shop in America.

Today, that's exactly what you get when you wander into Laishley Park and Marina in Punta Gorda.

It's now a tourist destination.

Harborwalk Scoops & Bites received national attention when TripAdvisor named it the No. 1 ice cream shop in the United States.

"In the dog days of summer, there's no better relief from the heat than a cool scoop, and the TripAdvisor community has helped identify the best ice cream shops that are worth a visit," Brooke Ferencsik, director of communications for TripAdvisor, stated in the press release. "Located 25 miles north of Fort Myers on Charlotte Harbor, this coastal ice cream shop serves more than 20 heavenly homemade flavors, including 'Captain Rum Raisin,' 'Toasted Coconut' and 'Chocolatey Chocolate Chip.' According to a TripAdvisor reviewer, 'The ice cream was delectable and creamy. The experience was enhanced by the idyllic location on a pier where some breathtaking yachts were docked.'"

Harborwalk Scoops & Bites wasn't a secret to Yolanda Marion of Charlotte Harbor.

"I love it," she said. "I like the convenience. I like the view. Everybody is very pleasant."

Co-owner Claudia Thomas said the TripAdvisor honor has brought in new customers.

"It's still surreal," she said. "It's a gift from the sky. How else do you explain it?"

Harborwalk offers not only its homemade ice creams, floats, malts and shaved ice, but also vintage sodas.

Live Like A Tourist ... **While Exploring**

Where: Laishley Park and Marina. From Marion Avenue, make a right onto Nesbit Street and you will run into it. The Laishley Crab House, Creator's Touch Gallery and Harborwalk Scoops & Bites will be on your left. The park and splash pad are straight ahead.

Harborwalk Scoops & Bites info: 941-505-8880; *www.scoopsandbites.com*

Creator's Touch Gallery info: 941-575-0022; *http://thecreatorstouch.vpweb.com/?prefix=www*

Laishley Crab House info: 941-205-5566; Reservations can be made online at *www.laishleycrabhouse.com*

Some families bring their children or grandchildren, who then can wash themselves off by playing in the nearby splash pad in Laishley Park.

Ruth Richardson moved to Port Charlotte from Sarasota and took her kids, Peyton, 1, and Ayden, 3, to Laishley Park.

"This is my first time," she said. "I like it. This is nice."

Harborwalk also is a great place to go after dinner upstairs at the Laishley Crab House, which serves some of the best sushi in the area. There also are low-calorie and gluten-free meals.

Before going up the beautiful wooden stairs and entryway of the Crab House, visit Creator's Touch Gallery, where you may be greeted by friendly cockapoo, Kendall.

Co-owner Audrey Freshman's gallery, which displays work from an estimated 150 artists, has been open for several years.

To fully enjoy Laishley, I recommend experiencing it all in this order: Creator's Touch Gallery, Laishley Crab House, Harborwalk Scoops & Bites and then the splash pad... or a walk around Laishley Park to burn off a few calories, and then get some ice cream.

And in case you were wondering — or if you have an ice cream bucket list — the other top ice cream shops in the United States, according to TripAdvisor are (in order):

- Bellvale Farms Creamery — Warwick, N.Y.
- Dietsch Brothers Inc. — Findlay, Ohio
- McConnell's Fine Ice Creams — Santa Barbara, Calif.
- Scottish Highland Creamery — Oxford, Md.
- Island Creamery — Chincoteague Island, Va.
- Martha's Dandee Crème — Queensbury, N.Y.
- Brickley's Ice Cream — Narragansett, R.I.
- Woodside Farm Creamery — Hockessin, Del.
- Brown Dog Ice Cream — Cape Charles, Va.

Shell Factory, North Fort Myers

Florida has its shell-filled beaches, famous mice, spacemen and Gators (both kinds). But it also has Burmese pythons, pink-painted houses, a religious theme park, and Miami.

Florida ranges from quirky to downright bizarre. Californians can relate, but until they can claim Fantasy Fest, Hulk Hogan, Redneck Yacht Club, and Polk County, they're just like second cousins to the weirdo sticking out named Florida.

If only there were a museum-like place that housed all of Florida's zaniness. ... There is, and it's just south of Charlotte County.

Welcome to the Shell Factory, home of Florida kitsch, where you can find Burmese pythons, shells, sequined hats, parrots, bumper boats, more shells, a zebra named Ann Curry, lemurs, dinosaurs, pirates, more and more shells, Santa Claus, T-shirts, fudge... mmm, fudge.

Phew! That barely scratches the surface. Let's take a closer look at the various areas that make up the Shell Factory.

First, there's the retail store, which is what many people think of when they drive by the iconic sign on U.S. 41. in North Fort Myers. Think of it as a large store filled with all kinds of souvenirs: T-shirts, hats, beach towels, ornaments, jewelry, magnets, sea life figurines, candy, and, oh yeah, shells in all kinds of varieties.

Live Like A Tourist ... **While Exploring**

In the same area don't be surprised to walk into a room of stuffed animals (not the kind you cuddle in bed), a den of pirates and a huge Christmas store. There also is a shell museum (naturally) and includes an impressive replica of All Saints' Church in Wittenberg, Germany, made of shells.

The retail store takes a minimum of 20 minutes to walk around. It's easy to get distracted and turned around as there are always new rooms or sections to investigate. There's also an arcade, candy store and Subway.

A short walk across the parking lot leads to the Nature Park, where more than 350 animals live.

After exiting the reptile house with super scary snakes (not the technical name) and walking by the Gator Slough, you might wander into a Dinosaur Park, where you can see large dinosaur replicas and learn about the creatures.

For a midday break, be sure to grab lunch at Capt'n Fishbones. The restaurant also is kitschy with sea life adorning the walls.

There are daily specials such as all-you-can-eat fish fry. "All you can eat" equates to "bring a big appetite." I, unfortunately, did not bring such an appetite, so instead I opted for a cup of the award-winning New England clam chowder, which was very creamy and tasty. I also ordered a house salad, which was a very generous size.

If You Go

Where: Shell Factory, 2787 North Tamiami Trail, North Fort Myers
For more info: 239-995-2141 or *www.shellfactory.com*
Tips: Go to the website—*www.shellfactory.com*—and click on coupons.

After a little food fuel, check out the Arcade or the Fun Park, where you can play miniature golf or ride on paddleboats for a small fee.

Unlike many touristy places, the Shell Factory truly is great for all ages from toddlers to seniors. Because who doesn't need a shell nightlight?

St. Armands Circle, Sarasota

Sometimes there are places you take tourists, and yet never fully experience or appreciate on your own. Maybe you're too busy making sure Grandma is having

a good time. Maybe you're too concerned about whether it's too hot for your northern friends. Or maybe you're just too worried about everyone else.

St. Armands Circle is one of those places I often took visitors but never fully explored or enjoyed on my own.

The Sarasota-based St. Armands Circle is a one-of-a-kind attraction offering dining, shopping, history, beautiful art and landscaping, all within walking distance of the Gulf of Mexico.

Many know it for its fashionable shops: Chico's, Lilly Pulitzer, Tommy Bahama, White House/Black Market.

Be sure to stop in the locally owned stores too. Sports fans from New York to San Francisco can find something to their liking at The Stadium Gallery. Destination Florida offers Life is Good attire, in addition to a store packed with Sarasota/Lido Key/Longboat Key souvenirs and beach-themed decorations.

Others may be more aware of its numerous dining options, especially the famous Columbia Restaurant. You can't go wrong there… or at Cha Cha Coconuts.

But if you leisurely stroll around the grounds, without cousin Eddie, you'll start to see there's more to St. Armands Circle than its shops and restaurants.

Sure enough… I had never noticed the "Ring of Fame."

"The Circus 'Ring of Fame' recognizes those persons who have made a significant contribution to the art and culture of the circus. With dozens of inductees from around the world, the Ring of Fame began in 1987 as a way to honor world famous

Live Like A Tourist … **While Exploring**

circus performers and the rich circus heritage of the Sarasota area," St. Armands' website states. "Each year, Ring of Fame honorees are nominated by the public and voted on by former inductees. Each inductee is then honored with a bronze wagon wheel plaque, which recognizes their contribution to circus art and heritage and recognizes their 'sponsor.' The annual Ring of Fame ceremony is a veritable who's who in the circus world, as current and past performers gather to honor their peers."

We all know the Wallenda family — famous for their high-wire acts.

I didn't know about Harold Alzana.

"On a thin sliver of wire 60 feet above the ground, he performed more near-suicidal feats than any other wire walker in circus history. With the Ringling show, he danced, skipped rope, and walked where angels fear to tread, flirting with death twice a day from 1947 to 1965," his fascinating plaque states.

I also didn't know that Alfredo Codona was the "king of the flying trapeze."

Nor, did I know about "The Nerveless Nocks." "Their circus roots date back to 1840 in their native Switzerland where the family owned a circus," their plaque states. "They first thrilled American audiences with their daring Swaypole routine in 1954. Since then they have thrilled millions worldwide."

If You Go

Where: St. Armands Circle
Hours: Stores open at 10 a.m. Monday through Saturday, and by noon Sundays. Most stores stay open until 8 p.m. or 9 p.m., but some close early, the website states. Breakfast restaurants open at 7 a.m. seven days a week; other restaurants are open 11 a.m. to 11 p.m. seven days a week.
More info for updated times: *www.starmandscircleassoc.com/index.cfm*

While reading about the dozens and dozens who left an impact on the circus and Sarasota, it's easy to feel John Ringling's presence.

One of the more beautiful parts of St. Armands is the "Allegory of Sarasota, Its Seven Virtues," which was "conceived and designed by Edward Pinto... dedicated February 2, 2008, to John Ringling and countless others who created the cultural jewel of Florida," the dedication plaque states. The seven virtues — Music, Flora, Aristotle, Sculpture, Asclepius, Bounty and Amphitrite — are represented by seven beautiful white statues.

And because you aren't entertaining any visitors, taking care of their every need, you'll notice that Michelangelo "looks with approval over the 'Seven Virtues.'"

Don't save St. Armands Circle for loved ones and friends; savor it for yourself too.

Village of the Arts in Bradenton

It once was a drab, color-muted, generic area that could have been Anywhere, USA.

"It has changed so much," said Douglas Holland, who owns Jerk Dog Records in the Village.

Now, there's no mistaking the vibrant, Crayola-coated Village of the Arts in Bradenton, where even the sidewalks offer inspirational messages: "Shoot for the moon and land among the stars."

"It's pretty awesome," said Douglas, who along with his wife, lives and runs his business at the same location in the Village. "We've been here long enough to see it go from economically deprived and seedy… sketchy… and it's just amazing the difference.

"It's just been wonderful to see the changes in the neighborhood."

The Village of the Arts in Bradenton truly is a living, breathing, working, creative, passionate environment. In the Village, business owners don't compete against one another; instead, they support one another. Each truly wants to see the others thrive, and even suggests where to go and whom to visit.

The Village is made up of dozens of art galleries, specialty shops, restaurants and studios.

"The Artists Guild of Manatee is a nonprofit group formed in 1999 with a mission to build a community where artists live and work while enhancing quality of life and creating a harmonious environment," the Village's website states. "In the past 15 years, the Guild and the Village community have worked hard to make the Village of the Arts a thriving community of residents and business that support the creative spirit… The Village is a residential neighborhood with a commercial overlay that creates a true live/work/play mix."

Even the "open" signs are friendly in the Village.

Douglas' record store (and home) is one of the many fun, distinct specialty shops. There are some albums known to the mainstream, but Douglas said he

specializes in what he calls "garage punk." The store has studio space for bands to perform during the Artwalk Weekend, which is a monthly event.

Artist Sally and Don Anderson Cosgrove first moved to Sarasota from Wisconsin a few years ago.

Live Like A Tourist … **While Exploring**

If You Go

Where: Village of the Arts, Bradenton. The boundaries are: from Ninth Avenue West to 17th Avenue West, between Ninth Street West and 14th Street West
When: Hours/days vary by business. Friday evenings and Saturdays seem to have the most number of businesses open.
More info: 941-747-8056 or *villageofthearts@gmail.com*

"We heard about this art area," she said of the Village, where "artists can live, work and sell their wares."

"It's really a fun, fun area to live in," she said. The couple live and work in Sally's Studio at12th St. W. Gallery. "We are going into our third year," she said. But, Sally noted, they felt like they had already found a family in the Village after just a few weeks.

Because the Village is a breathing, living, working community, some of the stores and galleries open to the public only a few days a week. The map of the Village, which is available online, indicates most businesses are open Friday evenings and Saturdays.

Each business owner takes great care of his building. Even when businesses are closed, it's fun to walk around the Village and appreciate the efforts and the artwork. You might find a large cow grazing in one yard, or a tree adorned with religious-themed art.

The Village isn't a snobby art place, either. It has more of an "everyone's welcome/carefree/utopian/altruistic" vibe.

Those looking to heal the soul can go to The Village Mystic, where karma beads, oils and other goods are available. Shaman Jeff Wheeler is on hand and he is a "talented medium and clairvoyant and connects with both his spirit guides and your spirit guides who share information and insights for you," his website states. "Jeff's philosophy is one of empowerment: it's your life, your divine purpose, and your choices. His goal is to share insights that help you clarify your own path to joy and fulfillment, and to help you recognize and develop your own gift of intuition."

He possesses two Dropa Crystal Skulls, which are "made of solid topaz, these life-size crystal skulls, dated between (8,000) and (12,000) years old, coming from a remote mountainous region in Mongolia. The Dropa Crystal Skulls are male and female, Za-Ka and Az-Ka respectively, meaning Integrity and Purity," his website states.

The Village Mystic also offers special opportunities for children as well. The Mystic Mines is located behind The Village Mystic, where kids can become prospectors and mine for gems.

The Village is a great half-day to full-day adventure... depending on how much you like to shop, walk, observe, appreciate and interact with the thriving, beautiful community.

Live Like A Tourist ... **While Exploring**

Worden Farm, Punta Gorda

Chris and Eva Worden could have gone anywhere.

They both have master's degrees in horticulture from the University of Maryland. They both have doctorates. Chris' degree is in crop science from the University of Connecticut, while Eva's is in ecosystem management from Yale University.

They could have stayed up north, establishing cool organic farms there. They could have taken their extensive knowledge and education to the Miami area, where Eva grew up and has family.

Instead, they developed an 85-acre U.S. Department of Agriculture-certified organic farm off Bermont Road in the eastern portion of Charlotte County, where they also are living, raising their children and preserving some of the land.

"We're feeding people healthy food and we're working with nature and providing jobs to people that are enjoyable and gratifying," Eva said.

To say they've put down roots here would be both literal and kind of funny to word-nerds.

Worden Farm has been featured on "The Nightly News with Brian Williams," "America's Heartland," "Florida Travel+Life," "Florida Trend," and other publications. They also "are recipients of the Florida Innovative Farmer Award, and have been named Organic Farmer Experts by the Organic Trade Association," states their website.

So what's the difference between a regular farm and a USDA-certified organic farm?

"Organic is a labeling term that indicates that the food or other agricultural product has been produced through approved methods," states the USDA's website.

Live Like A Tourist ... **While Exploring**

"These methods integrate cultural, biological and mechanical practices that foster cycling of resources, promote ecological balance and conserve biodiversity. Synthetic fertilizers, sewage sludge, irradiation and genetic engineering may not be used."

Here's just one example that separates the Worden Farm from non-organic farms: Tomato stakes that have been chemically treated may last longer, but the chemicals can leach into the soil and thus into the tomatoes.

If You Go

Where: Worden Farm, 34900 Bermont Road, Punta Gorda
When: Private tours are available. Contact office at *wordenfarm.com* to set up a tour.
Tips: Join the mailing list on the website: *www.wordenfarm.com*
More info: *www.wordenfarm. com* or 941-637-4874

Unlike at other farms, here you'll find dill and cilantro growing beneath tasty tomato plants. First, it's a space saver. Second, the aromatic herbs help deter insects and other pests.

"It looks more like a giant garden, and there's a lot of diversity," Eva said.

The Wordens may be providing healthy, organic foods to our community, but they're also providing jobs and educating the community.

There are several workshops offered at Worden Farm that promote healthy lifestyles. The following are workshops that have been offered: "What Do I Do With All These Veggies?" "Organic Gardening," "Food Preservation," "Small-Scale Livestock" and "Cheesemaking." Keep an eye on the Worden Farm's website or sign up for their newsletter for more information on these workshops.

Worden Farm also offers a membership program which provides a certain amount of produce for 20 weeks during season (December to April).

Those who are not members can still obtain Worden Farm produce at these farmers markets:

- Downtown Sarasota Farmers Market—Saturdays
  (October through May), at Main Street and Lemon Avenue.
- Saturday Morning Market in Downtown St. Petersburg. Saturdays
  (also October through May) at the Al Lang Stadium Parking lot at
  First Avenue South and First Street.

Worden Farm is not open for public tours, but private tours are offered. It's a very interesting and educational opportunity — perfect for community groups, service organizations, field trips, etc. To set up a tour or to get more information, email the office at *wordenfarm.com*.

... On An Adventure

Babcock Wilderness Adventures, Punta Gorda

It's like a safari, Florida-style.

Babcock Wilderness Adventures offers entertaining open-air bus (buggy) tours of Babcock Ranch, where tourists can see too many animals to count. Dozens and dozens of alligators, turkeys, turtles, cattle and birds of various kinds were among the animals witnessed during an educational 90-minute tour in Eastern Charlotte County.

First, a little history behind one of Southwest Florida's most important families and their land:

Edward Vose Babcock bought 156,000 acres of land in 1914 and founded the Babcock Florida Company. His son, Fred, later transferred 65,000 acres to the state, which became part of the Fred C. Babcock/Cecil M. Webb Wildlife Management Area. That left about 90,000-plus acres known as the Crescent B. Ranch.

Tour guide Peggy Dantuono put the size into perspective.

"That's about twice the size of Washington, D.C., and about six times the size of Manhattan," she said.

The Babcock Crescent B. Ranch became a working cattle ranch in addition to sod farming, timber harvesting and vegetable growing. Even the bees are busy at Babcock, making mild-flavored honey that's available for sale in the gift shop.

In 2006, the family and developer Kitson & Partners reached an agreement.

Kitson sold about 73,000 acres to the state, and plans to develop the remaining 18,000 acres for a private residential development.

"(The state's purchase) represents one of the single largest purchases of conservation land in the state's history," according to Florida Fish and Wildlife Conservation Commission. "The

Live Like A Tourist **... on an Adventure**

Preserve protects regionally important water resources, diverse natural habitats, scenic landscapes and historic and cultural resources in the rapidly developing Southwest Florida corridor."

Babcock Wilderness Adventures teaches you about the history of the ranch, which is far more fascinating than the brief summary just mentioned (find out what the ranch's doctor would do for an extra quarter). The guides, like Peggy, are so entertaining you won't even realize you are learning about Babcock's influence on the state's economy, environment and history.

Mike and Kathy Milak, of North Port, brought their son and his family from Montana for a Babcock Wilderness Adventures tour.

"I thought it was fantastic," Mike Milak said. "I never knew such a thing existed so close to home."

The wildlife, of course, is the highlight of the tour.

Peggy expertly drove the open-air bus (which once was a school bus) over bumps and between trees without clipping or hitting anything, helping counter the stereotype that women are worse drivers. She does it while sharing interesting stories about the ranch, and spotting wildlife (like a red-shouldered hawk).

There were enough visible alligators to fill a football team even if two of the gators were blocking each other (or, if you don't like the Gators-blocking-each-other joke, feel free to insert your own joke here). Jokes aside, one alligator even walked right by a venue of vultures and in front of the bus.

Guests also will see plenty of cattle during their tour. Some even will approach the bus and accept snacks from Peggy.

Babcock is home to several endangered or threatened species including the Florida panther, Florida black bear, wood stork, Eastern indigo snake, crested caracara, Florida burrowing owl, gopher tortoise, and red-cockaded woodpecker, according to FWC.

The tour includes the Telegraph Cyprus Swamp, named because the telegraph lines had to be located around the swamp.

Before or after the tour, be sure to explore the museum, which was used in the 1995 Sean Connery film, "Just Cause." There's also a gift shop and the Gator Shack restaurant.

Carve out a half-day for this adventure at Babcock Ranch.

Biking Boca Grande

I'm not a biker — not the "Easy Rider" kind, nor the "Breaking Away" kind.
I like air bags, not leather.
I like sparkles on my toenails, not road rash on my legs.
I like Spanx, not Spandex.
And thus, I'm not a biker/bicyclist.

But I do like riding a bicycle... at my leisurely pace, on a wide-open path with no cars around so I can pretend I'm a kid again on a mission to see friends and eat ice cream before it drips down onto the paper-covered cone.

I wanted that feeling again, but there was no way this nervous Nellie was going to feel that carefree riding along U.S. 41, or any other local roads for that matter. I understand this is a bicycle-friendly community and a lot of effort and money has been dedicated to this mission. Kudos to all. This truly is one of those: "It's not you, it's me" moments.

For the casual bicyclist/ nervous Nellie like me, there is a place where we can ride carefree... and it happens to be one of my favorite locations on Earth: Boca Grande.

In addition to the turquoise waters and quiet beaches, there is a wide 6.5-mile paved path on the island that is perfect for the amateur bicyclist. Of course, real bicyclists also can use the bike path.

Live Like A Tourist ... **on an Adventure**

"The bike/golf cart path and an accompanying jogging/walking path are part of Florida's Rails-to-Trails project, utilizing the old railroad right of way that carried phosphate to the southern tip of Gasparilla Island a century ago," the Boca Grande Chamber of Commerce's website states. "These days it provides passage for bikers, joggers and golf carts."

The Rails-to-Trails program has created more than 700 miles of trails in Florida, including the 6.5-mile Boca Grande Bike Path — the first such project in the Sunshine State, according to the Rails-to-Trails Conservancy.

The path provided stress-free riding as I cruised along, enjoying the sea breeze. I got a little nervous initially when a golf cart passed, but every driver waved and smiled — a common practice all over the friendly island.

"Golf carts are allowed on the bike path, but must give right of way to bikes and pedestrians," the chamber's website states.

I've been all over Gasparilla Island by car, but a bicycle allows you to quickly stop and photograph wildlife, like the non-native iguanas.

Because the island isn't East-Coast crowded, bicyclists can wander onto side streets and truly enjoy the canopy of the famous Banyan Street.

The bike path takes riders to the Gasparilla Island State Park, which is home to the Port Boca Grande Lighthouse.

Bicyclists can access the beach for free via the numerous public-access areas on the island.

And the best part of bicycling Boca? Easy parking. Simply pull into a bike rack — such as the one behind the Loose Caboose — and enjoy lunch and shopping at Fugate's, Boca Grande Outfitters, Gasparilla Outfitters and other local stores.

Because of Boca's bike paths, I could be that happy, carefree kid again on my bike looking for ice cream. And, of course, there's homemade ice cream on the island... though in this heat, it's definitely going to drip... and that's OK too.

Birding

Martha was alone when she died.

At one time, however, there were so many Marthas that they blackened the skies when they migrated along the East Coast.

"In 1860, one flock estimated to be a billion-birds-strong was said to be 300 miles long; it took 14 hours, from sunup to sundown, for the flowing river in the sky to pass," states the report, "The State of the Birds 2014."

Martha, the last surviving passenger pigeon, died Sept. 14, 1914, in the Cincinnati Zoo.

More than one hundred years later, she remains a symbol of what happens when we ignore our environment and neighbors.

The annual "State of the Birds" report focuses on bird populations that rely on one primary habitat, and therefore the report focuses on birds in "oceans, coasts, inland wetlands, forests, aridlands and grasslands, as

Live Like A Tourist **... on an Adventure**

well as species found on Hawaii, Puerto Rico and the U.S. Virgin Islands, and other U.S. island territories," it states.

The report indicates mostly good news for wetlands, coasts and grasslands since the original 2009 report.

The 2014 report lists "233 bird species most in need of conservation action." Bird species are most threatened in Hawaii, which has the highest rates of modern bird extinction, due to loss of habitat and introduced species.

"Among continental U.S. bird species, more than half of all shorebirds (sandpipers and plovers) are on the Watch List because of their small global populations and tendency to concentrate in small, threatened habitats during their long-distance migrations," the report states.

The winter/early spring months are the best time of year to see some of the endangered or threatened birds in Southwest Florida. Here are a few of the area's excellent, publicly accessible locations for bird-watching:

Charlotte County

Charlotte Flatwoods Environmental Park, 15801 Tamiami Trail, south of Punta Gorda: This is a large, 487-acre park, operated by Charlotte County and located near the Charlotte County Landfill. There are a variety of birds visible here due to its varied terrain. Visitors may see birds of prey and wading birds. Sightings may include: red-shouldered hawks, the rare red-cockaded woodpecker and sandhill cranes.

Bring water, binoculars and/or a camera, and wear comfortable shoes as there are lengthy trails. I didn't notice any mosquitoes, but bug repellent probably isn't a bad idea.

Nearby, on Zemel Road, is the Charlotte County Landfill — also home to an amazing rookery of birds. Wood storks, endangered in the United States, have been seen in large groups, alongside other birds and even a large alligator.

"Wood storks breed in the Southeastern United States, and are the only stork to breed in the U.S.," according to National Geographic.

Ollie's Pond Park, 18235 Avon Ave., Port Charlotte: This is a small neighborhood park that includes an easy-to-navigate trail around a pond, where many kinds of birds reside. This is a good place for those who can't walk long distances. Birds that have been spotted here: herons, grebes, ducks and egrets.

The park is dog-friendly, but please clean up after your pet.

Live Like A Tourist ... **on an Adventure**

Cedar Point Environmental Park, 2300 Placida Road, Englewood: This park offers both land and sea birds, as it sits on Lemon Bay. Migrating white pelicans could be seen flying over the park.

The park offers hiking trails, picnic areas and a visitor's center.

For more on birding in Charlotte County, go to *www.charlottecountyfl.com/ CommunityServices/NaturalResources/Birding.*

Sarasota County

Venice Area Audubon Rookery, 4002 S Tamiami Trail, Venice: For those who can't walk far, this is the best place to go. It's also one of the best to see nesting birds.

This is a small island in a pond, per se, but the island is essentially a condominium for birds. There are different species of birds nesting in different areas. The "island" also is patrolled by alligators — making it the one-stop shop to take northerners who want to see birds and gators.

For more on the rookery, go to *http://veniceaudubon.org/rookery.*

Myakka River State Park, 13208 State Road 72, Sarasota: This is one of the best places for seeing birds and other kinds of wildlife. If you have one day to take an out-of-towner to see Florida wildlife, make this your stop. Visitors are almost guaranteed to see alligators, herons, ospreys, egrets, anhingas, cormorants, etc.

The park is large, but visitors can drive to the park's main attractions. Some walking is still required — especially if the park is crowded.

Be careful leaving the park: I've seen deer alongside S.R. 72.

For more on Myakka River State Park, *www.floridastateparks.org/myakkariver.*

DeSoto County

Brownville Park, 1885 N.E. Brownville St., Arcadia: This is a great park for camping or fossil hunting. There is wildlife here, but it can be hard to spot. I did see a hawk and a cardinal. If the park is crowded, it may be harder to spot birds or other wildlife.

For more information on DeSoto County parks, go to *http://desotobocc.com/ departments/parks_recreation.*

Live Like A Tourist ... on an Adventure

Lee County

J.N. "Ding" Darling National Wildlife Refuge, 1 Wildlife Drive, Sanibel Island: "Ding" Darling is home to 245 species of birds, including the "big five" famous ones known to draw visitors: white pelicans, roseate spoonbills, reddish egrets, mangrove cuckoos and the yellow-crowned night heron.

Don't go on a Friday, when Wildlife Drive is closed. Any other day of the week is good. Be sure to wear comfortable shoes, and bring a camera and/or binoculars.

For more information, go to *www.fws.gov/refuge/jn_ding_darling.*

Six Mile Cypress Slough Preserve, 7751 Penzance Blvd., Fort Myers: This is a spectacular park that offers incredible views from a 1.2-mile boardwalk, which is open from dawn to dusk, seven days a week. There also is an interactive center, which has more limited hours.

For more information, go to *www.sloughpreserve.org.*

Live Like A Tourist ... **on an Adventure**

Cabbage Key

Like many of you, after moving down here, I heard about this magical island where Jimmy Buffett wrote his famous "Cheeseburger in Paradise." The island, Cabbage Key, was nearby and served cheeseburgers worthy of a song.

The only problem: Cabbage Key is accessible only by boat. I don't have a boat. I guess one could probably reach the island by helicopter or seaplane, but my aircraft have been in the shop (as in someone else's shop... and yes, someone else's aircraft). Thus, no "Cheeseburger in Paradise" for me.

The good news is that other people have boats, and King Fisher Fleet out of Fishermen's Village in Punta Gorda offers service to the island.

King Fisher Fleet is a great way for the boat-less, airplane-less, helicopter-less

to experience Cabbage Key.

Capt. Bob Navin and Mate Jim Miller greeted those of us boarding the vessel. There is plenty of cushioned seating available in the sun and in the shade. Nonalcoholic drinks and snacks are available for sale, but many of us carried in a bottle of water.

Capt. Navin makes guests feel at ease with his sense of humor and knowledge during the two-and-a-half-hour voyage, which includes a stop at Cayo Costa. King Fisher Fleet also offers service to Cayo Costa, and those guests will be dropped off on the way to Cabbage Key and picked up on the way back to Punta Gorda.

The boat departed at 9 a.m. and slowly moved into Charlotte Harbor while Capt. Navin provided information about the history of Punta Gorda and wildlife. Relaxing music (Bob Marley, the Grateful Dead, the Doobie Brothers) played at the perfect level to serve as the background soundtrack, allowing us to talk to one another and enjoy the view.

Within 90 minutes, we already had enjoyed two close encounters with pods of Atlantic bottlenose dolphins, who showed off by surfing in the boat's wake. I also caught glimpses of two sea turtles surfacing for air.

Live Like A Tourist ... on an Adventure

Where: Cabbage Key Inn Restaurant, Cabbage Key

How to get there: King Fisher Fleet offers transportation: *http://kingfisherfleet.com* or 941-639-0960

More info: 239-283-2278 or *www.cabbagekey.com*

Tips: Bring dollar bills to sign and tape on the wall; if you have your own transportation or plan to spend the night, make dinner reservations ahead of time.

After 13 years in Florida, the sight of dolphins, turtles or manatees never fails to excite.

The Cabbage Key Inn is the destination where Jimmy Buffett is rumored to have written the song. The restaurant is a beautiful white building on a slight, lush green hill surrounded by palm trees. There is outdoor seating for those wanting the constant water view. For a quirky, somewhat cooler view, go inside where patrons traditionally sign and tape dollar bills all over the walls and ceiling.

The menu isn't expansive because, after all, almost everyone there is ordering a big juicy cheeseburger.

Have a seat, take a deep breath (if the boat didn't relax you already), and enjoy eating a cheeseburger in paradise. After lunch, take some time to walk around the island on the trails, and be sure to climb up the water tower for amazing views of nearby islands, including the exclusive Useppa Island.

Be sure to try the Key lime pie, which is served frozen, in case you skim over that word on the menu (I'm not admitting that I did this, but I will admit to now reading more carefully so that I don't order something moldy). Save money on the fruity drinks (way too much for the size and not worth it). As for the cheeseburger, it was good, thick and juicy, and served with cole slaw or potato salad.

The truth about the cheeseburgers, however, is that Jimmy Buffett didn't write his song about Cabbage Key. He had endured rough seas on his way to the British Virgin Islands. The ice had melted. He was down to canned foods, peanut butter and thoughts of cheeseburgers. He reached the island and went to the restaurant at the end of the dock, where they happened to serve… cheeseburgers.

"The overdone burgers on the burned, toasted buns tasted like manna from heaven, for they were the realization of my fantasy burgers on the trip," states Buffet's Margaritaville website. "That's the true story. I've heard other people and places claim that I stopped or cooked in their restaurants, but this is the way it happened."

So that's the real story, but you can still get a cheeseburger in paradise at the Cabbage Key Inn… even if it isn't THE "Cheeseburger in Paradise."

Charlotte Stone Crabs, Port Charlotte

I can't tell you how many times I've seen "Field of Dreams," but I can tell you I've cried every time.

Warm tears blur the father and son having a catch in that Iowa field.

There's another moment that gets me every time too. It's when James Earl Jones' character, Terence Mann, delivers the beautiful, eloquent monologue about baseball in America:

"And they'll watch the game and it'll be as if they dipped themselves in magic waters. The memories will be so thick they'll have to brush them away from their faces. People will come, Ray. The one constant through all the years, Ray, has been baseball. America has rolled by like an army of steamrollers. It has been erased like a blackboard, rebuilt and erased again. But baseball has marked the time. This field, this game: It's a part of our past, Ray. It reminds us of all that once was good and it could be again."

That's just part of the monologue, but it gets me every time because it's so very true.

Football may have become America's favorite sport, but it's not as easy to play in backyards or in streets. Sure, you can throw a football around, and maybe even run a few routes. But without helmets and pads, you can't really play pickup football games with neighborhood kids.

That's the beauty of baseball. It's simple.

All you need is a bat, ball and glove. You don't need bases. The crack in the curb is first base. The sewer cover is second. The palm tree is third. The end of the driveway is home. That's how the game started for many of us: warm, sunny summer afternoons with kids in the neighborhood. You played for hours, pretending to be the greats of the game.

Sure, the game has changed. But at its core, it's still a lively ball teasing batters, seemingly winking as it whizzes by and into the chalky cushion of the catcher's mitt.

Live Like A Tourist **... on an Adventure**

Going to see a Charlotte Stone Crabs game is about as close as you can get to experiencing everything that's still great about baseball.

The players still have dreams of making it to the big leagues, and they play like it — diving, sliding, winging it, pulling an oblique muscle trying to foul off that outside pitch.

They wear their pants where baseball pants belong — at the knee — and not in a baggy bunch at the ankle like an old woman vacuuming the house in sweatpants.

They play in the heat, the humidity, the Florida evening rains... because it's summer, and that's when baseball is played best.

The Charlotte Stone Crabs have done an excellent job preserving what's great about the game while satisfying modern-day fans.

You can still get a hot dog, but you also can get cod fries. You can enjoy cotton candy, or MiniMelts. And you can wash it down with a Budweiser or a Mike's Hard Lemonade.

They offer entertainment off the field as well.

Carson Moore of Rotonda spent his ninth birthday at a game, where he had fun with friends on the playground.

If You Go

Where: Charlotte Stone Crabs game at Charlotte Sports Park, 2300 El Jobean Road, Port Charlotte

Cost: Prices vary. Tickets can be purchased through Ticketmaster or at the box office.

Box office number: 941-206-4487

Brenda Douglas and her son, Josh Newton of Port Charlotte, competed in a dance-off on top of the dugouts. Josh won, but Brenda still had a good time.

"It's a great atmosphere," she said. "Everyone's been friendly and nice."

John Cox brought his 3-year-old son, Conor, to a game during their six-week stay in Venice.

"The ball park is beautiful," said John, of England. "This is very impressive now. I like it a lot."

Conor wore his Wil Myers Rays shirt. John proudly wore his Rays shirt too. But on the back, where the player's name normally goes, John's read "Dad." The number, of course, one.

As the father and son walked from center to right field, the sun shared its final golden rays of the night.

"It reminds us of all that once was good and it could be again."

Cultural Center of Charlotte County, Port Charlotte

What do President Ronald Reagan, former first ladies Betty Ford and Barbara Bush, five Florida governors, author Stephen King and Cubs manager Joe Maddon

have in common? The Cultural Center of Charlotte County.

See? All the cool kids hang out at the Cultural Center.

The center has drawn visitors to Port Charlotte for more than 50 years. It has evolved from an adult-education center, called Port Charlotte U, into a one-of-a-kind complex offering shopping, entertainment, dining, events, conference space and fitness, in addition to education. It is a place year-round residents, snowbirds and tourists visit for its unique opportunities.

Shopping

The Cultural Center, a nonprofit, makes some of its money through its stores. Donated goods are accepted and sold through the Thrift Store, where one can find almost anything to furnish a home or fill a closet. Forks, spoons and knives can be found for 25 cents. Mugs and glasses also can be found for prices ranging from a few quarters to a few dollars. If your library needs books, there are plenty of soft- and hardcover books for sale as well.

Music lovers can find CDs for $1, and vinyl connoisseurs can sift through stacks of records, which sell for 10 cents apiece, unless marked otherwise. Sure, there are some polka albums in there, but I spotted the Carpenters, as well as some soundtracks. There also are plenty of Christmas albums available as well.

Speaking of Christmas, there are Christmas clothes for sale in the apparel department. Now, I'm not going to judge anyone's taste in style, but, in addition to some beautiful holiday shirts… let's just say someone looking for something to wear to an ugly Christmas Sweater Party might want to check out the racks.

Again, I'm not passing judgment… just offering a possible suggestion for an affordable snowflake-covered vest. And, purchasing clothes at the Cultural Center only helps the Cultural Center — and isn't that in the spirit of Christmas?

The Thrift Store sells nonholiday clothes too, of course, in addition to shoes, belts, purses and jewelry.

Live Like A Tourist … **on an Adventure**

The Boutique area of the Thrift Store offers higher-end dresses, coats and suits.

Those looking for collectibles or unique items may find what you're looking for in the Country Store. I spotted an old typewriter, a saxophone and a globe.

The Gift Shop is where you'll find one-of-a-kind, handmade items, such as quilts, stuffed animals, wall decorations, etc. All are made by the Happy Helpers volunteers, and, again, the profits go back to helping the Cultural Center.

Entertainment

There's something fun for everyone at the Cultural Center.

For those looking for friendship and games, the center offers a variety of games throughout the week. For example, chess players can challenge one another from noon to 4 p.m. Tuesdays and Thursdays. Dorothy Ladd and Bill Walker, both of Port Charlotte, were engaged in an intense match.

If You Go

Where: Cultural Center of Charlotte County, 2280 Aaron St., Port Charlotte
More info: 941-625-4175 or *www.theculturalcenter.com*

"That was dirty," Bill told Dorothy after her move. "Good," she replied.

A few minutes later... "You've won," Bill conceded.

Nearby, Carole Drake, Gina Adamo, Merry Devine and Barbara Palombo sat at a table playing mahjong. That game, too, is offered twice a week on Tuesdays and Thursdays. New players shouldn't feel intimidated. Herman Kalmaer will offer lessons. "I will not charge and I will not accept a gratuity," he said.

For a complete list of all games offered, go to *www.theculturalcenter.com/card-games.html*.

Theater

The Cultural Center's Theater, which seats about 500, has been home to some of the area's finest entertainment. For a list of upcoming entertainment events, go to *www.theculturalcenter.com/upcoming-events.html*.

Dining

The Cultural Center's restaurant, which used to be dated and drab, is now called the Beaches Cafe. It has a fresher, perkier, more Florida-like appearance, with the same affordable, good food available.

It's a perfect place to grab a bite to eat while shopping, playing games or taking a class — all of which benefits the Cultural Center, also known as "The Place that Friendship Built." Or, as I like to say, the place where the cool kids hang out... ya know, like Ronnie, Betty and Babs. OK, they didn't all hang out together, but you never know who you might meet and what you might find at the Cultural Center.

Live Like A Tourist ... **on an Adventure**

Geocache

Jim Finch can watch as cachers and muggles mingle from his desk. Some will need to use, "OYNPX." Others will later type, "TFTC."

Some of you are among the 6 million people around the world who know what all of that means.

The rest of you are muggles, and that's OK. I once was a muggle, too.

Jim, general manager of the Charlotte Harbor Event and Conference Center and a fellow Leadership Charlotte classmate, introduced me to geocaching — a modern-day treasure hunt using GPS. A cacher goes to www. geocaching.com to find nearby geocaches (or "cache" for short). He then types the GPS coordinates into a GPS device or GPS-enabled phone, and begins the search. Once found, the geocacher will go back online and log the cache on the website. Many will write "TFTC," which stands for "Thanks For The Cache."

"I got into it," Jim said. "I've always been into maps, puzzles."

Jim isn't a casual cacher (short for "geocacher"). He has found about 2,200 caches. "I have completed a challenge where I have found a treasure in every county in Florida," he said.

A cache may be a small tube holding only a log sheet. Or, it could be a large container filled with trinkets (toy soldiers, plastic dinosaurs, bracelets, etc.) in addition to a log book. "If you take something out, you are supposed to put something back in," Finch said.

Jim manages nine caches, including the Punta Gorda Travel Bug Hotel. Its location near Interstate 75 makes it a great place for trackable items like travel bugs or geocoins. These are items that contain a unique tracking number that can be logged into the website so their movements around the world can be tracked online. Some travel bug owners have goals for their bugs such as reaching a certain number of states or countries. The website defines geocoins as "a special coin created by individuals or groups of geocachers as a kind of signature item or calling card." Those also have unique tracking IDs so they can be followed on the website.

Jim took me to eight cache sites in the Punta Gorda area, including his Punta Gorda Travel Bug Hotel where I found no real bugs.

Some caches may be in remote locations, where no one likely would see what you are doing. Others, however, are hidden in plain sight. If you have been to Laishley Park in Punta Gorda, the

Live Like A Tourist ... on an **Adventure**

U.S. 41 bridges over Charlotte Harbor, Charlotte Sports Park, Englewood Beach, Tree of Knowledge Park in Arcadia, Myakkahatchee Creek Environmental Park in North Port... you've been near a cache and had no idea because you are a muggle, which is a non-cacher. The term is likely familiar to those who have read the "Harry Potter" books, in which a muggle is someone with no magical skills.

"Usually this term is used after a non-geocacher looks puzzled after befriending a geocacher searching for a cache, or when a non-geocacher accidentally finds a cache," states the website. "Geomuggles are mostly harmless."

Some caches include warnings, such as this one near an Englewood beach: "An easy cache in a popular high muggle area."

So how many caches are out there? More than 2.5 million worldwide, states the website. It's quite popular in Southwest Florida. A 25-mile radius search of the ZIP code 33950 (downtown Punta Gorda) reveals 1,720 caches. The same radius search of the North Port ZIP code 34287 and the Englewood ZIP code 34223 resulted in 1,799 and 1,750 caches respectively.

For the snowbirds, geocaching is happening up north as well. A 25-mile radius search of the lower Manhattan ZIP code 10004 produced 5,016 results. The ZIP code search for Skydeck Chicago (in the Willis Tower, which most of us remember as the Sears Tower) showed 8,407 caches and for Boston City Hall produced 3,352. For the Canadians, there are more than 44,000 in the province of Ontario.

It's a great hobby you can do while vacationing as well because it's something you can do while seeing the sights. Unlike some hobbies, caching can be accomplished in an hour or in a day. It's up to you. There are caches all over the Caribbean. For those going on a cruise this season, be sure to go online and get the coordinates before you depart so you can save on Wi-Fi costs. Europe, also, is practically covered with caches, according to the website's map. "They're all over the place," Jim said.

It's easy to get started at *www.geocaching.com*. Pick a user name (I chose FeinFinds). Pick out a cache location, type in the coordinates and have fun hunting.

GEOCACHING

What is it: A treasure hunt using GPS **How do I pronounce geocaching?** It sounds like "geo-cashing." **What do I need?** A computer or smartphone to access the website, and a GPS device or a phone with GPS. I might also recommend water, comfortable hiking/walking shoes, mosquito repellent if you plan to search in parks, wooded areas, etc. **How do I get started?** Go to *www.geocaching.com* **What are some words/acronyms I need to know?** If you just learned that LOL and OMG are not government-related acronyms, be sure to check out this site to learn the lingo.

Live Like A Tourist ... **on an Adventure**

Haunted History Tour, Fort Myers

There are bodies beneath McGregor Boulevard in Fort Myers. Not just a few, either.

There's a schoolmarm who continues to appear in a window of her old school.

And there's something bloody and terrible that happened a long time ago in a hotel.

These are just some of the stories you will hear during the Haunted History Tour in Fort Myers.

Tour guide Linda Farmer led a fascinating tour beneath a full moon in downtown Fort Myers, where she somehow turned old buildings into breathing, living storytellers of their own.

Linda, a Cape Coral native, begins the tour by asking the attendees to have an open mind. She further explains that, in order for a story to be shared on the tour, it must have been told by three people or from a credible member of the paranormal community.

The tour begins at the Franklin Shops, 2200 First St., which also is the first stop on the walking tour. Franklin Shops underwent a massive renovation from 2006 to 2010.

"One of the best ways to wake up a ghost... is to mess with its home," Linda said.

People have heard footsteps on the stairs, and some even have seen a man standing on the second level, where Walter Franklin originally had an office above his hardware store.

"There's a strong energy inside that shop," Linda said. "We do say goodnight to the man who never closed up his shop."

Linda then took us to a local hotel, where she said a wealthy man's mistress was rumored to have drowned during the hurricane of 1926. Some say her screams still can be heard out front by the pillars, where her body was found after the storm, Linda said.

Live Like A Tourist ... **on an Adventure**

The well-known Robb & Stucky building was another stop, where Linda said the first three floors were showrooms in the 1923-built structure. The fourth floor served as a sewing room, and supposedly the sounds of sewing machines can be heard at times, she said.

There were other stops with gory, ghoulish tales, but I don't want to share too many of those, or else you won't go on the tour.

But there's one more I'll share, because it probably affects you if you've driven McGregor Boulevard.

While crews were digging up shells to pave McGregor, they came across skeletons. They feared they came across an old Indian burial ground, which would have stopped their project. A doctor claimed the skulls did not appear to be of any Indian descent, but likely were Europeans or pirates. And so they continued building the road, using the shells and bones.

"There are 108 skeletons literally paved into McGregor Boulevard," Linda said.

No one knows what happened to the man in charge of that project. Some say he disappeared.

"Be careful who you pick up hitchhiking on McGregor Boulevard," Linda cautioned.

The tour is wildly informative and entertaining. Guests are encouraged to bring and use cameras, with hopes of capturing orbs or other aberrations.

Downtown Fort Myers offers many great restaurants and shops, so turn this into a great date night adventure.

For those who are concerned about whether you can hear the tour guide on busy streets, fear not (fear the ghosts more), as she wears a microphone.

If You Go

What: Haunted History Tour in Fort Myers
When: 8 p.m. Wednesdays and Saturdays
Where: Tours begin and end at Franklin Shops, 2200 First St., Fort Myers
Tips: Wear comfortable shoes and bring a camera. If the mosquitoes are still biting, bring some repellent. Also, bring cash to tip your tour guide and for parking.
More info: *www.truetours.net* or 239-945-0405

Mike Greenwell's Bat-A-Ball & Family Fun Park, Cape Coral

We've all heard it: "There's nothing for kids to do in Southwest Florida."
Hogwash. Pigclean. Boarbath.

Mike Greenwell's Bat-A-Ball & Family Fun Park offers a day full of fun for kids and families.

Mike Greenwell is a former Boston Red Sox player from North Fort Myers who opened the family fun park in Cape Coral more than 20 years ago.

"Growing up in Lee County he realized the need for a fun safe place for the kids of our community," states the website. "Since February 1992 Mike Greenwell's Bat-A-Ball & Family Fun Park has been Lee County's choice for family fun."

A day at Mike Greenwell's can include miniature golf, batting cages, Go-Karts, feeding dock, arcade games and the newly renovated Dugout restaurant. The

great thing about Mike Greenwell's is that there is no entry fee. You only pay for the activities in which you want to participate.

"We have people that just come to bat. We have people that just come to golf, so you don't have to do everything," said manager Dana Waters, who has been with Mike Greenwell's since the beginning.

The staff takes good care of all attractions as well.

The miniature golf course received new greens (carpets) for all 19 holes.

Mike Greenwell's also upgraded its Go-Karts, which are now ThunderVolt Go-Karts.

"These electric powered go-karts are packed with all kinds of features to maximize your riding experience," states the website. "Karts include an on board audio system that adds accelerator sensitive stock car engine sounds, headlights that activate for the duration of your race, and an all new sound

system in our go-kart pit that gives a play-by-play of the current race to spectators."

There are Go-Kart tracks available for various ages and skill levels:

Live Like A Tourist ... **on an Adventure**

- Junior track — small oval track for kids 52 inches tall or shorter.
- Slick track — large oval with karts that can drift. This track is for anyone 48 inches or taller.
- Grand National track — larger track with small turns and hills. It is for those 54 inches and taller (Phew! I'm tall enough). Double cars also are available on this track for an adult with a small child.
- Figure 8 track — This track offers two Go-Kart options: ThunderVolt or Sprint cars. The ThunderVolt Go-Karts run at two speeds. "Speed 1 is for children 8 years of age or old and 48 inches or taller," states the website. "Speed 2 is for children 10 years of age or older and 52 inches or taller."

Prices vary based on the track and car, but all rides are about five minutes.

If You Go

Where: Mike Greenwell's
Bat-A-Ball & Family Fun Park,
35 NE Pine Island Road,
Cape Coral
Cost: Depends on the activity.
Check out prices per attraction here:
www.greenwellsfamilyfunpark. com/attractions.html
More info: 239-574 4386 or
www.greenwellsfamilyfun park.com

If you want to be like Mike Greenwell, try out your skills in the batting cages. Speeds range from 30 to 75 mph.

For those who don't like sweating, fresh air or physical activity, head indoors to the 6,000-square-foot arcade. A Play Pass card system has been implemented, replacing the outdated token system. The card system can be loaded with money, which then can be used to play games in the arcade or ride the Go-Karts.

"It keeps track of everything," Dana said. For example, if you lose the tickets you win in the arcade, your card will remember how many you have earned.

The arcade is filled with both modern and classic games — perfect for family members of all ages. There also is an area for birthday parties.

The restaurant, Dugout, has been expanded from 40 seats to 180, Dana said.

"The menu is going to be to die for," Dana said. "Mike's picking out everything himself."

Upgrades also include adding a full liquor bar, more televisions and the NFL package.

An estimated 200,000 people visit Mike Greenwell's each year, Dana said.

So there's nothing for kids to do in Southwest Florida? Swinesoak.

Nav-A-Gator Grill & Marina, Lake Suzy

Many people know Nav-A-Gator Grill & Marina for its tasty burgers, good, live Trop Rock and its fun, laid-back environment.

The Nav-A-Gator also offers an interesting Wilderness River Cruise, where guests will see wildlife and learn about the plants, trees and history of the Peace River.

A captain led about two dozen of us on a 90-minute tour during a cool, windy afternoon. The captain kindly doled out blankets to those who were wearing shorts (aka northerners) and we slowly backed out of the marina, which is "the oldest, continually operating marina on the Peace River," he said.

"We're about 10 miles from the 75 bridge… Charlotte Harbor is about eight miles to the Gulf, so we're about 20 miles from the Gulf of Mexico," he said, helping orient visitors to the area.

The roomy pontoon seats about 40 passengers who can bring drinks from the Nav-A-Gator, which offers easy-to-carry beer buckets that are great for groups.

The captain has been leading these tours at the Nav-A-Gator since October 2012.

"We're going on our third year," he said.

Many, including me, wondered what kind of wildlife we might encounter.

"It all depends on what Mother Nature decides to put out," he said.

And Mother Nature was feeling generous that day.

The captain first took us to a bird rookery occupied by brown pelicans and roseate spoonbills, which is the beautiful pink bird with the spoon-like beak. The roseate spoonbill — an actual snowbird that winters down here — has an average wingspan of 50 to 53 inches, making it a magnificent sight in flight.

He also found several alligators, which were camouflaged along the banks where they could sun themselves and hide from the wind. The captain educated the passengers about the species and its difficult life cycle.

Live Like A Tourist ... on an Adventure

The wilderness tour ventures into the Peace River and around Liverpool Island. Who knew we had an island named Liverpool? Well, it turns out, we also had a town named Liverpool that once was home to about 60 people, according to former *Sun* columnist Lindsey Williams. Remnants of this town, founded by John Cross, can still be seen by the bricks lining parts of the river that once served as a dock. He also had a hand in creating Punta Gorda.

"Cross arranged the sale of a 30-acre town site (now Punta Gorda) from James M. Lanier to Col. Isaac Trabue of Kentucky in 1884," Williams wrote. "As agent for the Florida Southern Railway then pushing south from Lakeland, Cross helped persuade the company to extend its line to Trabue's property. Cross continued to broker sales in Trabue (Punta Gorda), bought many lots himself, and served as trustee for an annual chess tournament there endowed by the sale of pineapples. In appreciation, Trabue named a principal street for Cross (now Tamiami Trail, U.S. 41 south)."

I had no idea that was the origin of Cross Street and I've been living here for about 15 years.

The captain also shared interesting information about John Cross' influence in the Englewood area as well.

Cleveland resident Amy Trotch and her family experienced the wilderness tour during their vacation.

"It was excellent, especially if you aren't familiar with the area," said Trotch. "I would do it again."

I would do it again too, and I'm familiar with the area. The wilderness cruise is a fun way to see and learn about the Peace River. Those who have a larger group or special event can book a lunch cruise.

The Nav-A-Gator, in Lake Suzy, also offers affordable airboat rides.

For reservations or for more information about the Nav-A-Gator's river adventures, restaurant or cottages, call 941-627-FISH (3474) or go to *http://nav-a-gator.com.*

Paddleboarding, Englewood

Somehow, sometime in the last few years, people began standing on the water.

They used to sit in boats or kayaks, but now some of them stand on these cool, long, surfboard-like objects.

I had to try it, too. I had to be one of the cool beach kids standing on the water in one of the coolest new sports: stand-up paddleboarding.

The first thing you need to know is an important word: SUP. It's not like the greeting 'sup, although I guess you could say 'sup while standing on a SUP to other SUP-ers, but you might sound like a columnist who is trying a little too hard to be cool. SUP means stand-up paddleboard.

Nicole Miers-Pandolfi offered to introduce me to paddleboarding, or SUP.

Nicole runs her own paddleboarding company, SUP Englewood.

"I have had a love for paddleboarding for many years," said the Lemon Bay High School and University of South Florida graduate. "I would always come (to Englewood) to paddleboard."

The two most amazing parts about paddleboarding? The workout and the view.

I know your next thought is one of the following: "I'm not paying for a workout," or "There's no such thing as a fun workout," or "I thought this was supposed to be about 'living like a tourist,' not living like an athlete."

The workout part is as hard as you want it to be.

"I like the activity. I like to be physically active," Nicole said. "It's also a wildlife experience you can't get from a kayak."

I was skeptical about the view part. I've kayaked for several years, mostly in the Peace River and Charlotte Harbor. How can a few vertical feet make that much of a difference? It does (even from my less-than-average standing vantage point).

There's nothing else like it. You stand on a board above the warm, gentle, clear waters that reveal dolphin fins speeding by, lounging manatees poking their funny snouts up for breaths, alien-like blue crabs swimming sideways and shadows of rays skimming the bottom of the sea.

Live Like A Tourist ... on an **Adventure**

What: Paddleboarding

Where: Englewood and Venice are good areas, offering beautiful waters and wildlife.

Tips: Wear sunscreen and bring water. Also, consider getting a waterproof camera or a waterproof case for your phone, because you never know what wildlife you'll see.

Info: *www.supenglewood.com*

"There's so much beauty in Englewood," she said.

Nicole operates mostly in the Englewood, Venice and Nokomis areas. First-time paddleboarders should consider taking one of the tours offered because the tours include instruction on the land and in the water.

Englewood SUP offers tours near Boca Grande, Don Pedro, Casey Key, Stump Pass and North Jetty. If you prefer to be on your own, Englewood SUP also rents boards. She will bring the boards to you as well.

"We don't let people just pick them up," she said.

"It's so nice for people to not worry about pickup."

Now, for the most important question: Did I actually stand up and paddle? Yes. It's far more sturdy than I expected. Ten minutes later, I forgot I was standing on the water until I saw some clear blobs known as jellyfish. (Because that's when you mentally tell yourself, "Don't fall now," and then all you can think about is falling, so you start wobbling a bit.) It's also easier to stand up, sit down, climb on and climb off than it is to get in and out of a kayak.

Nicole has been working with Charlotte and Sarasota Special Olympics athletes.

"They went from never having been on a paddleboard to being able to stand up and paddle on their own," she said.

Paddleboarding also is quite safe, especially if you pay attention to weather conditions and know your limitations.

Of the 5,900 vessels involved in accidents reported by the U.S. Coast Guard in 2012, only four involved a stand-up paddleboard. Three of those were caused by weather or hazardous waters. The fourth was attributed to improper lookout.

Of the 651 deaths, only three were paddleboarders.

The boards Nicole uses for clients are 12 feet long and 31 inches wide — large enough to provide stability. "Literally anyone can do it," she said.

There are several local companies offering paddleboard rentals or tours. "It's really expanded in this area," she said.

Be sure to try this new, growing sport. It's truly an amazing way to explore the beautiful blue waters along the coast.

Peace River Charters, Arcadia

Many of us drive across the Peace River with little thought about the waters below that brim with life and history.

The 106-mile river flows from northern Polk County into the Charlotte Harbor Estuary.

There's a small stretch in DeSoto County you can explore via airboat with Peace River Charters.

"There's a lot of history here," said Captain Zac Varner, owner of Peace River Charters, during a tour.

Captain Zac stopped the loud whizzing airboat to share interesting stories about the Seminoles and their leader Osceola. He also may glide over land or into a 360-degree turn.

Captain Zac tailors his tours based on the guests' wishes. Some tours may incorporate more history; others, more thrill.

Seasonal North Port residents Catherine and Glen Alton enjoyed their first ride so much, they brought fellow Canadian friends Carol Chambers, Randy Van Ness and John Galloway.

"It was awesome," said Catherine. "I saw more wildlife this time."

A maximum of six guests board the airboat and put on noise-reducing headphones.

Captain Zac then revs up the motorboat, and off you go into the great wild of the Peace River.

Southwest Florida Water Management District offers a section on its website that provides interesting information about the river and the Charlotte Harbor Estuary:

Live Like A Tourist ... **on an Adventure**

- "Its waters are a dark brew of leaf detritus, organic acids and tannin, distilled from the peaty soils of the wetlands and forests through which it flows."
- "To the Seminole Indians, who settled on its banks two centuries later, it was Tallackchopo, 'The River of Long Peas,' for the wild peas that covered the river's banks."
- "In 1881, Captain J. Francis LeBaron of the U.S. Army Corps of Engineers discovered phosphate while surveying the Peace River south of Fort Meade. Additional deposits were discovered in 1886 by John C. Jones and Captain W.R. McKee, who quickly formed a company and commenced mining operations. In 1888, Captain T.S. Moorehead created the Arcadia Phosphate Co., purchasing the rights to mine sections of the riverbed. Within a decade, over 200 companies were mining phosphate in central Florida, and the price of an acre of Peace River land had soared from $1.25 to $300."

Wouldn't it be amazing to find an acre for $300, let alone for $1.25? I'll sign that dotted line today!

Captain Zac also points out wildlife along the river, especially the 11-foot gator they call Rosco.

Common animal sightings may include alligators, raccoons, white-tailed deer, armadillos, turkey and various kinds of snakes and turtles. Expect to see lots of birds as well. Our group (me and the Canadians… sounds like a movie) saw a great blue heron and a bald eagle.

"It was so beautiful," Carol said of the hour-long tour.

Black bears and panthers, though rare, do wander into the Peace River watershed on occasion, according to Southwest Florida Water Management District.

Captain Zac and two other captains provide tours at various times throughout the week. Private, group and custom tours are available. Reservations can be made online (*http://peacerivercharters.com/*) or by calling 863-444-0693.

If You Go

Where: Peace River Charters, 4135 SW Adventure Way, in Arcadia

Tips: Don't wear chunky, dangling earrings as you'll have on headphones. Also, if you wear a baseball cap, plan on wearing it backward or you may lose it in the river. Wear sunscreen.

More info:
http://peacerivercharters.com/ or 863-444-0693

Live Like A Tourist ... **on an Adventure**

Pure Fort Myers River Cruise, Fort Myers

Many residents of Charlotte, DeSoto and Sarasota counties are familiar with the Peace and Myakka rivers.

Just a short drive is the Caloosahatchee, where urban life and nature coexist while the lapping waves remind us of the river's historic importance to the region.

Pure Fort Myers offers a fascinating River Cruise aboard the Edison Explorer boat.

Capt. Marty Martino, along with First Mate Jim O'Neal, not only safely guides guests along the river, but he also serves as a master naturalist — thereby providing information about the mangroves, palm trees, dolphins, manatees, wood storks and other wildlife.

The tour begins by slowly floating by the Edison and Ford Winter Estates.

"Seeing this property (from the river) is the exact way Edison saw it in 1885," said Phil Chase, site historian for the Edison and Ford Winter Estates. That's right, Pure Fort Myers includes a historian aboard the Edison Explorer.

Edison bought 13.5 acres of picturesque waterfront property.

"He came down here to escape the cold," Phil said. (Don't we all!)

Ford and Edison became friends, and they had winter homes next to each other on the Caloosahatchee.

"These two men would literally change the way we live," Phil said.

110

The River Cruise continues back toward the downtown as guests learn about the Calusa Indians and the Union's fort in the Civil War.

"You gave me a lot of information I didn't know," Maine transplant Beverly Caraven told Capt. Marty.

From downtown, Capt. Marty steers the boat beneath the historic Railway Bridge and by two bird rookeries — one of which was filled with nesting wood storks. The endangered birds would fly to one island, snag a twig, and return to the rookery where the active nest-building mirrors the Interstate 75 bridge expansion in Fort Myers (though with less traffic and heavy machinery, of course).

Fellow guests aboard the Edison Explorer saw an eagle, dolphin, pelicans, woodstorks, roseate spoonbills, herons and other birds as well during the 90-minute cruise.

The River Cruise is a great way to learn about the Caloosahatchee, but it also could be part of a fun, interesting day by working in a tour of the Edison and Ford Winter Estates with lunch or dinner at Pinchers Crab Shack, which is located at the marina.

Pure Fort Myers also offers sunset cruises, fishing charters and boat rentals.

For more information on the special events or on any of Pure Fort Myers' other adventures, call 239-919-2965, email info@PureFortMyers.com, or go to *www. PureFortMyers.com.*

If You Go

Where: Pure Fort Myers River Cruise, 2360 W. First St.
More info: *www.purefortmyers. com* or 239-919-2965
Tips: Take a camera or binoculars for wildlife viewing. Much of the boat is covered, but sunscreen is recommended regardless.

Live Like A Tourist ... **on an Adventure**

Segway Venice

I've been injured doing the following activities: walking on grass, scraping ice off the car, crossing a street, putting down luggage, walking on a sidewalk, opening a refrigerator and playing Nintendo.

So the idea of riding a Segway made me nervous. What if I fall off the Segway? What if I forget I'm on a Segway, step off and roll an ankle? What if I Weeble-Wobble and actually fall down?

But riding a Segway seemed fun and exciting, and therefore, I had to try it.

Segway Venice is a great way to experience a Segway while also learning about the city of Venice.

Maureen Kearns started her Segway business in 2009 in Detroit, where she continues to operate tours of the city from May to October. She brought the Segway touring company to Southwest Florida in 2011 and settled in Venice, where she offers Segway tours from Christmas to Easter.

Segway Venice provides three different tours available: the Nolen Plan Tour, the Legacy Trail Ride and the Intracoastal Ride.

The Nolen Plan Tour is "made for urbanites and history buffs," states Segway Venice's website. "We'll discuss the history of Venice and see historic buildings, residential districts and several parks, a tenet of John Nolen's city plan."

The tour lasts for about two hours and goes about three miles.

The Legacy Trail Ride covers about four miles in 90 minutes. This is the one geared for those who want to really ride the Segway and pick up some speed.

Live Like A Tourist ... **on an Adventure**

The Intracoastal Ride takes about two and a half hours, covering six miles. Ten percent of the ticket sales from this tour will be donated to the Venice Area Beautification.

"We'll ride from 41 to 41 on the island," states the website.

I went on the Nolen Plan Tour with tour guide Matt Clegg, who quickly put me and others at ease.

Riders first watched a safety video, which provided information about the Segway.

Matt then took us outside, where Chicagoan Mark Benko bravely volunteered to step on the Segway first.

"It's not very difficult," he said. "You get used to it pretty quick."

He's right. Everyone in our group got used to their Segway-legs, so to say. I didn't Weeble-Wobble off, nor did anyone else.

We drove our Segways along the Intracoastal Waterway, near Venice High School and residential areas while Matt educated us about the history of Venice, which included interesting stories about the circus, the train station and Mrs. Palmer who became a wealthy widow when her husband died.

"She was astronomically rich," Matt said. "She fell in love with the area. She bought 60,000 acres. She was the first snowbird."

Matt continued to talk about how Mrs. Palmer's influence led to the creation of the train depot in Venice. Riders also will learn about Venice's connection to World War II and the 9/11 attacks.

It's an interesting tour of the city on a fun mode of transportation.

If You Go

What: Segway Venice
More info: *https://detroitsegways.com*, or call 855-U-SEGWAY
Requirements: At least 14 years old, between 100 and 260 pounds, able to walk unassisted up a flight of stairs and not pregnant. Riders also must wear closed-toe shoes and the provided helmet.
Tips: Wear comfortable, closed-toe shoes as you will be standing for about two hours.

Seminole Casino, Immokalee

I always count my money while sittin' at the table, despite what Kenny Rogers says. Of course, I don't play with a lot of money so it's pretty easy to count a handful of chips.

You don't have to go to Las Vegas to enjoy a weekend at the tables while the luring beeps, boops, bings and cha-chings of slot machines play like a soundtrack of modern-day Sirens.

Seminole Casino in Immokalee — now called Seminole Casino Hotel — opened the 99-room hotel portion as part of a major expansion to the entire 175,600-square-foot complex.

The casino's expansion, which brought with it 100 additional jobs to Southwest Florida, includes:

- An 800-seat Seminole Center that can accommodate concerts, dances, conventions, etc. The stage area also opens outside, where 3,000 people can attend outdoor concerts. Comedian Ron White and KC and the Sunshine Band were among the first performers, which attracted thousands of fans.
- A new restaurant, Lucky Mi Noodle House. "Chefs will blend traditional ingredients with contemporary influences to create new interpretations for dishes such as Vietnamese Pho Noodle Soup, Thai Panang Curry Noodles with Malaysian Sauce, Japanese Dynamite Prawn Tempura, Korean Blugogi and Indonesian Shrimp," states information provided by Seminole.
- An outdoor swimming pool with private Seminole Chickee cabana units that can be rented.
- A 24-hour fitness studio.
- A 5,600-square-foot addition to the casino floor that now offers more than 1,300 slot machines. There also is a nonsmoking area now.
- A new Seminole Poker Room with six tables and large TVs.
- Nineteen suites, three of which are called Paradise Suites for high rollers. Those fancy suites include two iPads for guests to use during their stay.
- And speaking of high rollers, the Paradise High Limit Room

Live Like A Tourist ... **on an Adventure**

was improved to include a private restroom, 73 new slot machines as well as two midi-baccarat tables and 10 blackjack tables (for those who can afford to play $50 minimum tables).

Seminole Casino Hotel now offers an entire weekend's worth of entertainment. The Immokalee casino first opened in March 1994, making it a destination for day-trippers.

Guests can now enjoy alcohol beverages and spend the night in rooms that range from 450 square feet to 900 square feet. The rooms all come with flat-screen TVs, elegantly designed bathrooms and free Wi-Fi in addition to typical hotel amenities such as an ironing board, hair dryer, mini-fridge and coffee maker.

Room rates in the four-story hotel vary so call ahead or check online. There are four places to grab a bite to eat: EE-TO-LEET-KE Grill, 1st Street Deli, Lucky Mi and Cappuccino's.

Before you start gambling, be sure to visit the Player's Club and obtain a card for The Seminole Player's Club Wild Card Rewards Program. This allows you to earn comps while you play. Even if you don't bet a lot or play often, you may receive a $5 discount on food by signing up for the card.

If You Go

Where: Seminole Casino Hotel Immokalee, 506 First St.
When: Open 24 hours a day, 365 days a year
Tips: Get a player's card to earn comps. Gamble with money you can afford to lose. When it's gone, walk away.
More info: 1-800-218-0007 or *www.seminoleimmokaleecasino.com*

Table games includes: blackjack, mini-baccarat, midi-baccarat, three-card poker, Ultimate Texas Hold 'em, Pai Gow poker, Let It Ride, Blackjack Switch, Spanish 21, Mississippi Stud and Double Deck Pitch Blackjack, states the casino.

There are four pits for table games, and of course, the famous Zig Zag Blackjack Pit where the drinks are free and the "Blackjack dealers are hotter than the cards in your hand," states the casino.

Those who prefer the slot machines won't be bored. The slots range from 1-cent to $100. (Who can afford to put $100 in a slot machine for one spin?) The machines also vary from traditional cherries to high-tech, 3-D, interactive games.

"We try to do the newest slots," Baker said.

Whether you play penny slots or blackjack in the Paradise High Limit Room, know your limits. Take with you only the amount of cash you can afford to lose.

As Kenny Rogers sang, "Know when to walk away; And know when to run."

Live Like A Tourist ... **on an Adventure**

Shark Tooth Hunting

So a blonde goes shark tooth hunting and catches a fish… nope, that's not a joke. It happened.

Venice has been known as the "Shark Tooth Capital of the World," and therefore I had to go a-huntin' at Caspersen Beach.

I ventured out to the famed Venice beach, feeling like Elmer Fudd armed with a shark tooth shovel.

Immediately, something struck me as strange (stranger than an image of me with a musket and shovel saying, "Sssh, I'm hunting shawk's teeff,"), but I couldn't figure out why. A few minutes later, I realized the source of the strangeness: Everyone was engaged in the same activity.

Think about this for a minute. Usually at a beach there are some people sunbathing, reading, swimming, walking, shell collecting, snorkeling, skimboarding, building sandcastles, etc. Nope, not at Caspersen. Like one giant treasure hunt to which they all had invites, everyone had their shovels or sifting pans in a few feet of warm Gulf water.

Dig, sift, dig, sift, dig, sift.

So I grabbed my shark tooth shovel, also apparently known as a Southern snow shovel, and waded into the party.

Live Like A Tourist … on an Adventure

Where: Caspersen Beach,
4100 Harbor Drive, Venice
When: 6 a.m. to midnight,
every day
Tips: Bring a shark tooth shovel
and drinking water. Also,
consider bringing bug spray (the
no-see-ums can be annoying).
More info: 941-861-5000 or
parksonline@scgov.net

"The trick is to imagine where the tooth may be," joked Captain Greg Abbott of Sarasota.

The largest tooth Greg has found is about an inch.

"I'm still a rookie," he said.

Everyone, of course, is hoping for the jackpot.

"We're trying to find a megalodon tooth," said Sheena Guadagno of Venice.

"I'm looking for the megalodon," said Chuck Allen of Palatka.

The megalodon became extinct about two million years ago. They were about 60 feet long and had about 276 teeth at any given time, according to the Florida Museum of Natural History.

Chuck is not a rookie hunter.

"I try to come down here four or five times a year," he said.

Chuck loves searching for the teeth because they are so old.

"You're talking prehistoric," he said. "They're extinct."

Sheena also has been shark tooth hunting for a few years.

"It's just relaxing," she said.

It's a great activity for all ages. There are no lifeguards on duty at Caspersen Beach, so keep a close eye on the little ones (though you should always keep an eye on them whether there are lifeguards or not). This isn't the best swimming beach in the area. There are rocks and boulders in the water so consider wearing sandals or other water shoes.

You don't have to be a skilled hunter to find teeth.

I collected about a dozen over the course of several hours in addition to a fish... go figure.

Live Like A Tourist ... **on an Adventure**

Southwest Florida Skydive Club, Punta Gorda

Dear Mom and Dad,

I still have no tattoos or weird piercings, and I cannot relate to the women in "Orange is the New Black" — so please keep all of that in mind as you continue reading.

Let me also add that it's more dangerous to drive a car or eat food than to do whatever it is I might have, maybe, done. And it could be worse. I could have gone yak skiing, volcano boarding or extreme ironing (except that we know I don't/can't iron).

So… let's just get this over with: I may have, allegedly, reportedly jumped from a perfectly good airplane. Don't worry, I had a parachute, which seems kind of obvious now. And don't worry, I wasn't alone. I was strapped to a man I had never met. Hmm… that doesn't sound good.

But I assure you: It's safe. It's very safe. The employees at Southwest Florida Skydive Club take it very seriously, stressing safety from the moment we arrived.

Safety measures were addressed in a video, in writing and in person. The instructors taught the proper way to land (legs up) during a tandem jump. They also educated us on the proper body positioning during the free-fall. Jumpers even practice that form on the ground as well.

Mostly, the instructors maintained a relaxed demeanor, which immediately put me at ease. Roy Torgeirson, who was my instructor, isn't new to the field of skydiving. "I did my first jump July 4, 1974," he said. He has jumped about 7,000 times, and now averages about 350 a year.

Southwest Florida Skydive Club, owned by Anne Touron, first opened in LaBelle, but Hurricane Wilma destroyed it, Roy said. They reopened at Shell Creek Airpark, off Washington Loop Road, in 2006.

I'll admit to being a bit nervous. I looked up statistics on skydiving deaths prior to jumping. I was mildly comforted to know I was more likely to die from heart disease, cancer, motor vehicle crash, falling (not out of an airplane), choking, firearms and heat, according to the National Safety Council. Of course, then I started getting depressed at all the possible ways I'll likely die. So I might as well jump out of an airplane.

With the radio blasting that morning on my drive to Shell Creek Airpark, Tom Petty's "Free Fallin'" suddenly came on one of the stations. I took it as a good sign. Then, as I neared Washington Loop, Kenny Loggins' "Danger Zone" started playing, which I took

Live Like A Tourist … on an **Adventure**

as another good sign… until I remembered that Goose died in "Top Gun." But we weren't flying fighter jets that day, so it was still a good sign.

Typical summer storms delayed us a bit, but then it was time to walk to the plane. That's when it suddenly got real. We took off on the grassy runway and slowly climbed to more than 10,000 feet. Then the door opened and out I went… and that's when the first expletives may have been uttered.

But then, there I was, staring down at the building-dotted, street-slivered, waterway-woven earth. And it's beautiful. It's breathtakingly beautiful. I was floating at 120 mph, which makes no sense, but that's how it feels to free-fall. I was completely captivated by seeing the planet in a new way that I forgot I was hurtling toward it — until the parachute opened, literally yanking me back into reality.

We soared beneath the large parachute for about five more minutes (I lost track of time).

Roy taught me how to steer, and so I swung us to the left and to the right, while life continued in this great, big world. Below us in Charlotte County, in houses and offices, our neighbors were going about their days: typing on computers, washing dishes, playing Candy Crush, etc. Beyond the rivers I couldn't see, beyond the farmlands that extend for miles, there were residents of a town called Ferguson who no longer went about their normal lives. And beyond the oceans, there were other Earth-sharers who have never known a day as peaceful as mine was that morning in the skies above Punta Gorda.

Because storms had moved through the

If You Go

Where: Southwest Florida Skydive Club, Shell Creek Airpark, 36886 Washington Loop Road, Punta Gorda
When: Call for reservations
More info: 941-875-8554, *info@skydiveswflorida.com* or *www.skydiveswflorida.com/index.htm*
Tips: Wear comfortable, loose-fitting clothes as you will be in a tight harness (super-short shorts would not be comfortable). Wear sneakers or other sturdy, close-toe shoes. Don't wear jewelry that can whack you in the face or that you would be upset losing.

area earlier that morning, we were left with little breeze. Normally, skydivers land into the wind. For us, that meant we were coming in fast — a likely butt-landing. Roy guided us in for the landing at the airpark like the pro he is, gently sliding us to the ground as if we were kids gliding onto a Slip 'N' Slide.

I then kissed the ground, and not because I ever feared for my life. I kissed the ground because it was such an amazing, memorable adventure. I kissed the ground because I was feeling so very fortunate to be alive on this mysteriously wondrous planet. I kissed the ground because I want to be kinder to this beautiful Earth… to my home.

And I'm pretty sure that's something you both taught me, right, Mom and Dad? Treat the world well, and don't get tattoos, right?

Live Like A Tourist … on an Adventure

Sun Ride Pedicab & Historic Tours, Siesta Key

Siesta Key is known for its beautiful sugar beaches, its famous fried Salty Dogs and its cool drinks on hot nights.

The island off Sarasota also is known for interesting architecture, legendary tales and fascinating history that includes Al Capone's ties to Siesta Key.

Glen Cappetta offers a fun, unique tour of Siesta Key through his company, Sun Ride Pedicab & Historic Tours.

Glen pedaled away from 27 years in the corporate world and started the eco-friendly pedicab business with one bicycle about five years ago.

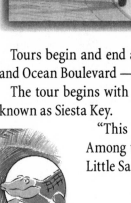

"It's been a labor of love," Glen said.

For those who don't know, a pedicab is a bicycle that tows a kind of carriage, in which guests can comfortably sit and enjoy the passing sights. Glen's company has pedicabs that can seat two to three adults comfortably, and larger ones that can fit a few adults and children.

Sun Ride Pedicab & Historic Tours offers free transportation around Siesta Key, which helps bar hoppers get around and motorists who often have trouble finding parking. Though the service is free, tips are accepted.

For those spending a day on the island, be sure to book one of Glen's Historic Tours.

Tours begin and end at the gazebo located at the intersection of Canal Road and Ocean Boulevard — in the heart of Siesta Key Village.

The tour begins with a little history of the island, which hasn't always been known as Siesta Key.

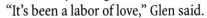

"This island has had a lot of different names," Glen said. Among the key's previous names: Clam Island, Muscle Island, Little Sarasota Island and Sarasota Key, he said.

Live Like A Tourist ... **on an Adventure**

The island looked far different in 1906, when Capt. Louis Roberts and Ocean Hanson Roberts opened the Siesta Inn. More people eventually took advantage of the peaceful island, which became a place to winter for the wealthy and famous including Charlton Heston, Cecil B. DeMille and Bette Davis.

Siesta Key's population grew from 31 full-time residents in 1910 to 24,000 in 2010, Glen said.

On the tour he explains how the bridges were built, as well as the canals. And he will pedal guests into the residential areas, where visitors normally don't venture. Some of the homes remain from the 1950s, most well-kept and beautiful. Others are newer and grandiose — the kind you expect on an island.

There's one home that's no longer there, however, that raised my eyebrows and morbid curiosity. Apparently, Al Capone's mother had a home right on the water (literally). Glen said the home had "two different docks — one for high tide and one for low tide." So in addition to rum running, of course my mind wandered to once-weighted down bodies of Capone's enemies now reduced to remains on the bottom of the sea as cruise ships sail above with happy passengers drinking rum runners.

Glen's tour includes a stop at the beach, which has been named one of the best beaches in the world for its fine white sand. There are theories about the sand, and also about a forbidden love, which some believe are the reasons the island hasn't been directly hit by a hurricane… but you should hear those stories from Glen.

He also gives a little information about the island's wildlife.

If You Go

What: Sun Ride Pedicab & Historic Tours
Where: Tours begin and end at the gazebo in Siesta Key Village, at the corner of Canal Road and Ocean Boulevard.
Reservations: 941-343-3400
More info: Call 941-343-3400, *www.sunridepedicab.com* or *info@sunridepedicab.com*

"There are no poisonous snakes," Glen said. Phew!

There have been a few bobcats spotted, and of course, a lot of birds.

Glen's Sun Ride Pedicab & Historic Tours is the perfect way to learn about the island while dining, drinking and enjoying a perfect sunset on the beach.

Live Like A Tourist … **on an Adventure**

Sun Splash Family Waterpark, Cape Coral

Kids always need a place to cool off while burning energy.

Sun Splash Family Waterpark in Cape Coral is a great place to take kids (especially younger ones).

Sun Splash offers 14 acres of pools, slides and splashes.

There are two large ones—Electric Slide and Power Surge—that take riders down five stories on single or double tubes.

There also are three tall, high-speed ones — X-celerator, Terror Tube and Thunder Bump — and riders must be 48 inches tall to go down (yes, I was tall enough).

There are a few other shorter water slides at the park as well.

There's enough to keep kids entertained, but older kids (teens, young adults) might get bored after a while. Adventure Island in Tampa may be a better option for more experienced water park fans.

Sun Splash is great for little ones, and those looking for lower-speed fun.

The Main Stream River Tube Ride, aka a lazy river, is always a fun, relaxing, quarter-mile trip around the park.

Live Like A Tourist ... **on an Adventure**

The Tot Spot seems to be a popular place, where little ones can play with squirting water and climb on fun playground-like equipment. There's the Rain Tree, which is more like a Rain Mushroom, where kids can stand beneath and get drenched. And then there's the Pro Racers, which appears to be the world's slowest water slide for little, little ones.

While there are vigilant lifeguards on hand throughout the park, there are a few things parents need to know:

- Lifeguards are not babysitters. Parents should not be sleeping or reading books. They need to watch their children.
- Know your child's limits. Don't exaggerate Jimmy's swimming ability as Phelps-like. Children do not understand the weight of water and how going down a water slide will force them several feet beneath the surface.

If your child can't swim, don't waste the money. If he plans to splash around and run through squirting water, save the money and take him to the splash pad at Laishley Park in Punta Gorda, or to a local beach. There, they at least can play in the sand while you keep those hard-earned dollars.

If You Go

Where: Sun Splash Family Waterpark, 400 Santa Barbara Blvd., Cape Coral
When: Check the website: *www.sunsplashwaterpark/hours/*
More info: *http://sunsplashwaterpark.com* or 239-574-0558

Treeumph, Bradenton

I'm a tree hugger.

Sometimes you have to hug a tree after traversing an elevated bridge made of swinging steps.

What better way to celebrate Earth Day than by hanging out in the trees... and sometimes hugging them... at Treeumph Adventure Course.

The Bradenton ropes and zip-line complex is a fantastic way to test your physical skills, bond with family and friends, forget about your troubles back on land and enjoy the bird's-eye-view from the trees.

For those who are unfamiliar, the course is made up of various ladders, bridges and zip-lines. That doesn't sound bad, right? Except that the bridges may be a wire cable, or netting, or moving steps. And it's all elevated in the trees — allowing you to swing like monkeys or soar like birds (awkward, goofy monkeys and birds, that is, if you are like me). You are, of course, attached to one or more cables and carabiners, and therefore you won't fall 60 feet to the ground.

Treeumph offers courses for kids and adults, based on age and reach.

Size requirements are as follows:

- Children's ticket: Ages 7-11, and kids must be able to reach 55 inches with both hands while standing flat-footed.
- Junior ticket: Ages 9-11, and kids must be able to reach 69 inches with both hands while standing flat-footed.
- Adult ticket: Ages 12 and older, who can reach 71 inches with both hands while standing flat-footed. Those who are between the ages of 12 and 15 need to be with a ticketed adult who is 16 or older.

Whether you are a child or adult, all participants must watch a safety video and successfully complete a small, close-to-the-ground course in order to demonstrate safety skills and confidence.

For adults, there are five courses you can attempt to complete. They become gradually more difficult. The Summit course is considered extreme, and most are unable to attempt it as it requires a lot of upper-body strength.

During my visit, I only had enough time to complete the first three courses and they were so much fun — and yes, tiring. I'll

Live Like A Tourist ... **on an Adventure**

be honest and admit that I was sore the next day… or three. But I definitely will return so I can at least make it through the fourth course.

At the end of your course, head to the "Treeumph ZIP-Line." This requires climbing a 60-foot ladder, but it's worth it as you zoom down the 650-foot zip-line.

Kathy and Aaron Corr own Treeumph, which they opened Jan. 12, 2013.

"We had moved to the area and were looking for a change of careers," Kathy stated. "The concept of this type of park was one that we had seen work very well in Canada, where we had lived before. We felt that with the population size, tourism numbers and the lack of outdoor activities that this idea would be a great fit for folks wanting to get out and be active. The ability to be open year-round was a great feature of the area as well."

If You Go

Where: Treeumph Adventure Course, 21805 State Road 70 E., Bradenton
When: Make reservations at *http://treeumph.com/tickets*, or by calling 941-322-2130.
Tips: Wear comfortable shorts and closed-toe sneakers/hiking shoes. Take mosquito repellent and water (though water can be purchased). Though you are in shade a lot, there are pockets of sunshine so be sure to wear sunscreen.
More info: 941-322-2130 or *http://treeumph.com*

The Corrs made a conscious decision to protect the environment when building Treeumph. "We use innovative construction techniques to protect trees and allow them to continue to grow naturally. Our innovative compression system safely secures platforms to trees without damaging them or infringing upon their continued growth and health, and allows sap to circulate freely," states the website, *treeumph.com.*

"We design our trails to protect the forest floor and minimize root damage. The system also protects the trunk from damage by using protective half logs and sheathed cables, which reduce cuts and deformation due to anchor tension.

"We also protect sensitive habitats like wetlands from damage."

At some tourist attractions, especially at amusement parks, trees and vegetation are torn down.

At Treeumph, the trees are the attraction.

"The trees and the environment are important to us for many reasons," Kathy stated. "We love the outdoors and want to be able to sustain and preserve as much of the natural setting in the world as possible. It is obviously important for the future of our and our children's ecosystems. From a business perspective the trees are an asset to us. We use the trees as part of our games so protecting them becomes even more important to us."

Live Like A Tourist ... **on an Adventure**

Useppa Island

Useppa Island, with its Caribbean-esque beauty and sirens-worthy history, lures guests and then bids them farewell with lottery-ticket fantasies.

The island is a private, members-only club, but that doesn't mean you can't experience that tax-bracket lifestyle… for a few hours.

Useppa Island is a short boat ride away from Gasparilla Island, nestled between Cayo Costa and Pine Island. Cabbage Key, also only accessible by boat, is slightly southwest of Useppa Island. In addition to a boat, however, you'll need to be a member or know a member (there are less than 1,000) in order to experience Useppa Island.

If you are in the market, "cottages" range from about a half-million to $2.95 million for the 3,000-square-foot Rum Cove Cottage, which has been featured on the televised "National Architectural Report," according to *http://useppa.com/real-estate/rum-cove-cottage/*.

If owning a "cottage" on Useppa Island isn't in your budget this year, there are 750 nonresident members who can get you on the island — including some boat charter companies such as Boca Boat Cruises, out of Boca Grande.

Kathleen Wolcott, longtime owner of Boca Boat Cruises, has been escorting guests to Useppa Island and Cabbage Key daily.

Guests greet Kathleen and her vessel, Katara, at a dock near the Pink Elephant restaurant. She and her captain provide interesting information about Boca Grande, Useppa Island and wildlife along the way.

The wildlife, however, stole the show during our trip.

Dolphins didn't just swim by to say hello. They jumped and

Live Like A Tourist … **on an Adventure**

flipped for several minutes at a time, giving passengers plenty of opportunities to take National Geographic-like photos.

"I loved the dolphins," said Louise Doyon of Parker, Colo.

Boca Boat Cruises also took guests by a small island near Gasparilla Island where a few thousand white pelicans crowded the sandy shore.

While many would consider leaping dolphins, feeding osprey chicks and flying, 30-pound white pelicans the highlights of the day (and it would be most days), Useppa Island truly is a remarkable sliver of paradise.

If You Go

Where: Useppa Island
How: Boca Boat Cruises
More info: *www.bocaboat.com* or 888-416-BOAT (2628)
More info on Useppa Island Club memberships:
239-283-1061
Tips: Bring sunscreen and a camera

First, there are no cars on the island. You walk. But it's more like a saunter... stop and look at an orchid... saunter some more... stop and look at the bright bromeliads. The path leading from the docks to the Collier Inn isn't a boring sidewalk. The island basically is a botanical garden.

The Collier Inn is the main, beautiful house in which you likely will eat lunch. It once belonged to Barron Collier.

The majestic, white inn overlooks Pine Island Sound, providing beautiful vistas for diners.

If you arrived via Boca Boat Cruises, you'll have time to explore the island's small museum. There, you will learn about Useppa's long, unusual history (from the Paleo-Indian people to the CIA and hurricanes).

Stroll around the island, which has a carpet-like croquet field and a large-sized, outdoor chess board.

For more information on Boca Boat Cruises trips to Useppa Island, go to *www.bocaboat.com* or call 888-416-BOAT (2628). For more info on membership to the Useppa Island Club, call 239-283-4227.

... In the Great Outdoors

Amberjack Environmental Park, Rotonda

Amberjack Environmental Park offers more than 200 acres of walking trails and boardwalks leading to Lemon Lake, where great blue herons, egrets, ducks and others frolicked together near a lounging alligator.

Bird-watching has to be the best activity at Amberjack Environmental Park. I'm not a bird expert, nor an ornithologist (such a fancy word), but I spent quite a while bird watching and taking photos at one of the boardwalks at Lemon Lake. Those interested should bring binoculars. Roseate spoonbills are known to frequent the park.

Those more interested in walking can find 5.5 miles of trails at the park. There is a map on the Charlotte County website indicating the trails by color. Forget the map. The trails aren't marked well so it's better just to scrap the idea of following a map, and instead go exploring. The trails are wide with little-to-no human traffic... making it a great, peaceful place for a stroll or a jog. There may be, however, animal traffic.

While wandering around the park, I heard a snort nearby. I couldn't ascertain if it was an alligator or a hog, and quite frankly, I'm glad I didn't see the face behind the snort or else my strange natural instinct of stomping, dancing and singing the Muppets' "Mahna Mahna" may have surfaced once again in public (this previously happened

Live Like A Tourist ... **in in the Great Outdoors**

at Charlotte Flatwoods Environmental Park in South Charlotte County and at Myakkahatchee Creek Environmental Park in North Port). I'm inclined to believe it was a hog (probably a large, salivating, greasy one with green horns and the attitude of a mother protecting her bacon bits). Parts of a trail looked like the Tasmanian Devil had been hiking, turning up the dirt along the way as hogs do in the wild. "Mahna Mahna."

If You Go

Where: Amberjack Environmental Park, 6450 Gasparilla Pines Blvd., Rotonda
When: Sunrise to sunset every day
Tips: Wear comfortable shoes, bring drinking water and binoculars. There are no bathrooms.

Amberjack, first created in 1994 and later expanded in 2004, is one of five environmental parks in Charlotte County (six if you count the two areas of Tippecanoe). The county also maintains five preserve areas, which are described as:

"Preserves are generally larger environmental parcels with less urban interface and sensitive environmental habitats that are important to the community and are the guiding influence for management," states the county's website. "Management of preserves will focus on environmental preservation and resources first and foremost with more intensive management and monitoring. Preserves have limited public use, less programming, and less structures/amenities."

Residents and visitors are more likely to visit one of the county's environmental parks, such as Amberjack.

"Environmental parks are typically smaller in size than a preserve, have more urban interface, and may have some sensitive environmental habitats that are less important to the guiding influence of management," states the county's website. "Management will focus not only on environmental preservation, but will also manage the natural resources from a human dimension. There may be less intensive management and monitoring in an environmental park; however there will be more public use, more programming, more interpretive features, amenities and multi-use trails."

The county offers several educational walks at Amberjack. One walk is specifically geared for bird-watchers while the other is designed for those interested in other areas of nature.

For more info on the walks or on the park, call 941-625-7529.

Bay Preserve at Osprey

Many tourists, and even some Southwest Floridians, drive through Osprey without stopping.

There are, however, several attractions including the Bay Preserve at Osprey, which sits on the picturesque Little Sarasota Bay.

The 4.3-acre site includes the beautifully maintained Burrows-Matson House, which was built in the 1930s. The estate is a popular site for special events and weddings.

"Bay Preserve at Osprey is right next to Historic Spanish Point, and many don't even know it's there (I didn't and I was born and raised here)," wrote Shauna D. on the popular wedding-planning site, *www.theknot.com*. "The property is large, open, beautiful and right on the water. You can have the nature-filled wedding that you wanted as you say your vows underneath the trees, or have your ceremony up against the water while the

sun is setting. The two-story historical house that we got ready in is absolutely beautiful! The staircase inside of the house is a must-have for pictures."

Those who are not getting married also can stroll the grounds or play checkers on a table near the bocce court.

The Honore T. Wamsler Wildlife Observation Platform allows visitors a chance to look for birds, dolphins and other wildlife in Little Sarasota Bay.

There is a kayak launch as well, but there is a bit of a hike from the parking lot to the water so make sure you can easily carry your vessel.

Bay Preserve at Osprey is protected by the Conservation Foundation of the Gulf Coast, which "works with landowners, businesses, and government to protect and preserve the beauty and natural

Live Like A Tourist... in in the Great Outdoors

integrity of the bays, beaches, and barrier islands," states the website. "The Foundation purchases natural areas, holds land preservation agreements, and educates for responsible stewardship. The Foundation also serves as the land acquisition agent for Sarasota County's acclaimed environmentally sensitive lands program, their neighborhood parks program, and is a partner in efforts to preserve Florida's natural heritage."

For more information on the foundation, go to *www.conservationfoundation. com.*

Bay Preserve is a beautiful place to visit, but it won't take all day to fully explore the waterfront estate.

Instead of driving through, or leaving Osprey after your visit, take advantage of the other naturally beautiful attractions in the Osprey/Venice area while visiting Bay Preserve.

Historic Spanish Point, 337 N. Tamiami Trail, Osprey

If You Go

This is an incredible 30 acres of preserved history and beautiful nature trails, also located on Little Sarasota Bay and within walking distance of the Bay Preserve. Expect to spend a few hours exploring the grounds, and especially the historic buildings and the archaeological exhibit, "A Window to the Past."

Where: Bay Preserve at Osprey, 400 Palmetto Ave.
More info: 941-9918-2100 or *www.conservationfoundation. com*

Oscar Scherer State Park, 1843 S. Tamiami Trail, Osprey

This 1,381-acre state park can be an all-day, or a partial-day adventure. Visitors can hike, swim, canoe, camp or picnic while enjoying wildlife.

Venice Rookery, 4002 S. Tamiami Trail, Venice

There is plenty of birding activity at the Venice Area Audubon Rookery, which is only a few minutes from the Bay Preserve. This is an excellent place for birders or for those who want to see wildlife, without having to walk more than a few yards.

Bok Tower Gardens, Lake Wales

Imagine a place where the flowers bloom in bright brilliance, where the bells ring out in a beautiful concert, where the mighty oaks offer shade with the help of Spanish moss curtains, where the squirrels run up to greet you and where the birds sing sweet serenades.

It sounds a bit Cinderella-ish, but it's an actual paradise here in the Sunshine State.

Bok Tower Gardens is in Lake Wales, which is in Polk County. Before you say, "That's way too far," let me reassure you, it's so worth the drive. There is nothing else like it in Southwest Florida.

First, there's the most obvious part of the 50-acre garden: the Singing Tower, a 205-foot focal point that houses the 60-bell carillon. The bells erupt in concert each day so check the times when you arrive.

"The bells are amazing," said Melissa Parish of Palm Coast. "The tower — it's a work of art that plays music."

Philadelphia architect Milton B. Medary designed the Singing Tower along with sculptor Lee Lawrie (the man behind the bronze Atlas at Rockefeller Center in New York City). The Tower is made of coquina, marble and ceramic tiles.

"I definitely was in awe," said Tiffany Snider of Pompano Beach, who was visiting for the first time with family. "It's bigger than we expected."

The entire complex is bigger, better and more beautiful than expected.

As you enter the gardens, you are immediately inspired and greeted by a saying from Edward Bok's grandmother: "Make the world a bit better or more beautiful because you have lived in it."

There is an orientation video first-time visitors should see before exploring. It plays in the Visitors Center, where you can learn more about the history of Edward Bok, the tower, bells and

Live Like A Tourist ... **in in the Great Outdoors**

garden. Be sure to check out the film and the center because they will further enhance your experience.

One of the interesting aspects is that Frank Law Olmsted Jr. worked as the landscape architect (even I have heard of him). He worked on the Biltmore Estate with his father, who designed Central Park. Olmsted Jr. "eventually landscaped many of Washington, D.C.'s most prominent landmarks, including the White House, Jefferson Memorial, Washington National Cathedral and the National Zoo," according to the Bok website, *www.boktowergardens.org.*

Have I convinced you yet that this isn't some run-of-the-mill garden?

Remember those Calgon commercials in which a busy, working mom with screaming toddlers gets in a bathtub and says, "Calgon, take me away." The gardens are basically a Calgon commercial.

The gardens and specialized exhibits are so beautiful it's difficult to figure out where to look and where to walk.

Two must-see parts of the gardens: Window by the Pond and the Endangered Plant Garden.

The Window by the Pond is almost like a nature theater. You walk into a small, theater-like box that has a large, well… window by the pond. It provides a front-row seat to look for birds, snakes, alligators, etc.

The Endangered Plant Garden is just what it sounds like as well. It's a circular garden filled with endangered plants.

Be sure to save a full day to explore all parts of Bok Tower Gardens. You can grab lunch at Blue Palmetto Cafe, which is located near the Visitors Center and the gift shop. Speaking of the gift shop, that's a must-do as well. You can find many one-of-a-kind items, plus a selection of plants to start your own garden.

If You Go

Where: Bok Tower Gardens, 1151 Tower Blvd., Lake Wales

Tips: Wear comfortable shoes, sunscreen and mosquito repellent. (I didn't notice a lot of bugs, but that may be because I had some on already.)

Also, Google "Spook Hill" and swing by on your way out of town. I don't want to ruin it for you, but it's one of those "only in Florida" quirky places. If you go (or if you have been there), and Spook Hill did its thing, let me know. The hill must have been napping when I arrived.

More info: *boktowergardens.org* or 863-676-1408

Of all the places I've been for the Live like a Tourist column, Bok Tower Gardens ranks way, way, way up high on my list of favorites. After all, it conjured up an image of Cinderella. That's how awesome it is. Now, if only a pumpkin-carriage could carry me there.

Calusa Heritage Trail, Pine Island

I thought Pine Island was just a cute little fishing community. I thought it was a good place to spend an afternoon, grab fresh seafood, and stroll the shops and galleries.

I was right, but I had no idea about the island's rich history until I visited the Calusa Heritage Trail at the Randell Research Center, which is a Florida Museum of Natural History program.

"The Calusa Heritage Trail is one part of the Randell Research Center," said Cindy Bear, coordinator of programs and services.

Researchers use the Pine Island center as a base to excavate and study sites around Southwest Florida. Among the research projects:

- Useppa Island: Results from an excavation conducted continue to be analyzed at the museum, which is located on the campus of the University of Florida.
- Mound Key (near Fort Myers Beach): Researchers were using ground-penetrating radar in an attempt to find structural remains from the Spanish and Calusa settlements.

"People lived here for a long period of time," Bear said.

Live Like A Tourist ... **in in the Great Outdoors**

The Calusa Heritage Trail, however, is a remarkably fascinating journey for guests to learn about the history of Southwest Florida.

"The Calusa were prosperous, powerful, and artistic Native American people whose homeland was Southwest Florida — today's Lee, Charlotte, and Collier counties," states one of the educational signs.

The trail is 3,700 feet of easy-to-navigate paths, with numerous, beautiful and informational signs educating guests about Calusa life.

"A combination of fresh water (from the Peace, Myakka, Caloosahatchee, and other rivers), the protection provided by barrier islands, and shallow, grassy estuaries of extraordinary year-round productivity contributed to Calusa success at fishing and shellfish gathering," states another one of the signs.

If You Go

Where: Calusa Heritage Trail entrance, 13810 Waterfront Drive, Pineland on Pine Island
More info: 239-283-2062; *www.flmnh.ufl.edu/rrc/*
Tips: Bug spray, bug spray, bug spray. Also, bring some drinking water.

Both the trail and center are located in the Pineland area of Pine Island, which is believed to have been one of the biggest communities for the Calusa.

"Calusa towns often featured high mounds, shell ridges, canals and broad, flat plazas," states another sign. "Larger towns (including Pineland) have similar layouts, often with twin mound complexes divided by a central canal. Given its prominence, architectural complexity and location at the entrance to the Pine Island Canal, Pineland may once have been the capital of the entire Calusa domain."

The trail isn't an all-day adventure. In fact, the trail can be walked and the signs can be read in about a well-worth-it hour. In that short time period, however, the mosquitoes can and will attack like alligators devouring a carcass thrown into their swamp. OK, maybe that's extreme, but if you go during the summer months, take a shower in bug spray and wear sleeves and pants.

After, check out the Tarpon Lodge nearby. Don't expect fast-food prices or taste. This is a very good restaurant with daily specials and homemade desserts. There are also several other restaurants on Pine Island as you head back toward the mainland.

Cedar Point Environmental Park, Englewood

You have to dip your feet into the water.

It's the law.

OK, so maybe it's not, but when you come into contact with a river, stream, lake, bay, harbor, ocean, etc., you have to take off your shoes. You can't live a full life without knowing how it feels when sand swallows your toes, or when a passing, dancing piece of seaweed tickles your ankle, or when a gentle wave rolls in with a larger-than-it-should-be splash as if to say, "Come on in already, the water's warm."

That's what happened at Cedar Point Environmental Park. One thing led to another, and there I was, barefoot in Lemon Bay. I was also happy and living life according to the rules of nature that dictate when shoes should be shed.

Cedar Point is located on a triangular piece of land bordered by Placida Road and Lemon Bay. The 115-acre park is smaller than some of the county's regional/ environmental parks, but it's packed with a half-day's adventure. I would recommend going in the morning to avoid the hot, afternoon sun.

If you have children who have that built-in radar capable of detecting the presence of a playground, steer them to the left of the Cedar Point Environmental Center and toward the trails. (Otherwise the day might be spent on a slide instead of trails.)

Informational signs state there are the following trees located in Cedar Point: Xeric Pine Flatwood, Mesic Pine Flatwood and Hydric Pine Flatwood.

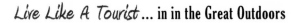

Live Like A Tourist ... in in the Great Outdoors

Where: Cedar Point
Environmental Park, 2300
Placida Road, Englewood
Tips: Be sure to check out the
Cedar Point Environmental
Center. Bring water and bug
spray.
More info: 941-475-0769

I couldn't honestly tell them apart in a lineup. (Not that there would ever be a tree lineup because what would a tree do? Have a bonfire within 10 "rods" of a house? That's an actual Florida statute. Is that like 10 guys named Rod lined up? I don't know any Rods, and I have never conducted a home-improvement project using such a measurement.)

Other park signs indicate Cedar Point is home to 18 species of mammals, 130 birds, 19 reptiles, 10 amphibians and seven fish species. Among the residents: gray foxes, raccoons, gopher tortoises, bald eagles, bobcats and the eastern diamondback rattlesnake (ooh, scary).

In a description of the bobcat, the sign states they likely will be "silently observing you before you see them." Well, that's a comforting thought. I kept looking over my shoulder, half-expecting a big, angry cat to jump at me like that scene in "Apocalypse Now."

There are six color-marked trails totaling 2.6 miles. The longest trail —yellow, which goes by the names Tortoise Trail and Crystal Trail — is only .65 miles.

I took the Tortoise Trail, which meanders through the pine flatwoods and meets up with the Crystal Trail, which veers along the mangroves. From there, I took the pink-marked Eagle Trail and cut over to the purple-marked Jeep Trail, which leads directly to Lemon Bay and one of the most peaceful places in the park.

There, a small wooden boardwalk takes you right into Lemon Bay. I couldn't be rude to Mother Nature, so yes, the shoes came off and the feet went into the warm water as a dolphin swam by the mangrove-lined park.

There are picnic tables scattered throughout Cedar Point, and since the trails aren't very long, it's possible to carry your lunch. Before you leave, stop inside the Cedar Point Environmental Center. There, you can look at shells and skeletons, and learn about other parks in the area.

There are many free fliers and handouts educating residents about everything from water conservation to wildfires. If you can spare a dollar or two, please donate to the center, which is operated by the Charlotte Harbor Environmental Center.

If you go, don't forget the most important thing of all: You have to dip your feet into the water.

Charlotte Harbor Environmental Center at Alligator Creek, Punta Gorda

I usually worry about 18-legged, venom-oozing snakes that have so many large, blood-dripping fangs they would be called alli-conda-monsters. This is what I picture every time I hear the rustling of a small lizard in some brush: alli-conda-monsters.

Once I pop jumbo marshmallows on the fangs in my imagination, I can enjoy Florida's wildlife. I can even learn a little, too. And I learned a lot during a free guided walk with volunteer John Fenton at the Charlotte Harbor Environmental Center at Alligator Creek.

John, a retired chemist and seasonal resident, began learning about Florida's flora a few years ago, and he now shares that knowledge with environmental center visitors.

"The coontie was, more or less, the major food of the Calusa," John said. "They ate seafood, too. They did tap the coontie."

The first person (or first few people) to try the coontie plant must have lost a bet or picked the short straw since the coontie actually contains a toxin.

"Spanish writings from the 16th century report that the original native Timucuan and Calusa people removed the toxic chemical, cycasin, from the coontie stem by maceration and washing," according to Daniel F. Culbert, county extension agent III, Cooperative Extension Service, Institute of Food and Agricultural Sciences, University of Florida. "They then used the starchy residue to produce a bread. This was an important food source that sustained them throughout most of the year."

The coontie, which looks like a fern, now is used more for landscaping — but keep it away from pets due to the cycasin toxin.

John also pointed out the psychotria nervosa wild coffee plant, which actually has no caffeine and doesn't taste good.

As we continued walking along the 1-mile Eagle Point Trail, John kept an eye out for poison ivy and explained how to identify it: three leaves and the middle one usually is the largest.

Speaking of poison, there's a plant in the wild far more dangerous than poison ivy or the coontie. There, on a vine, were clusters of red and black, berry-sized balls.

"This is abrin here — one of the most poisonous materials known to man," John said.

Abrin, which is commonly called rosary pea, jequirity pea or crab's eye, can be compared to ricin.

"Abrin, like the similar plant toxin ricin, causes toxicity by inhibiting the formation (synthesis) of proteins in the cells of the exposed individual," states the Centers for Disease Control and Prevention. "Abrin (and ricin) may cause severe allergic reactions. Exposure to even a small amount of abrin may be fatal."

A Lee County man pleaded guilty to "producing and selling potentially deadly toxins ricin and abrin for use as weapons and conspiring to kill a woman in the United Kingdom," according to the FBI.

Aside from the poisonous plants, there are many more nonpoisonous ones along with lots of wildlife at the environmental center.

Be sure to check out a free guided walk with one of the other environmental center volunteers. The free guided walks take place at several parks in Charlotte County. Check out the center's website for the calendar of events, where you can also find out about wading adventures, estuary pontoon boat journeys and other programs for adults and kids: *www.checflorida.org/Calendar.html.*

The Charles E. Caniff Visitors Center holds a gift shop and provides additional information. The center also is manned by volunteers. If you are interested in volunteering at the Punta Gorda site or at Cedar Point Environmental Park in Englewood, go to *www.checflorida.org/Volunteer.html.*

If You Go

Where: Charlotte Harbor Environmental Center at Alligator Creek, 10941 Burnt Store Road, Punta Gorda

Tips: Wear comfortable shoes that can get muddy (if it's rained recently) and mosquito repellent. Bring water, binoculars and/or a camera.

More info: *www.checflorida.org* or 941-575-5435

Corkscrew Swamp Sanctuary, Estero

"This is best/coolest/most amazing park."

I've said this sentence, or a variation of it, several times. But in reality, it's just not fair to compare the amenity-filled Lakes Regional Park in Lee County, to the beautiful Gulf waters of Stump Pass Beach State Park in Englewood, to the wildlife and canopy walk at Myakka River State Park to the bird lover's paradise at the Venice Area Audubon Rookery.

Parks are like stores: some are the big-box kind offering everything from groceries to socks to car parts, whereas others specialize in clothing, jewelry, sporting goods, etc.

Corkscrew Swamp Sanctuary, in North Collier County, fits the size of a big-box park: 14,000 acres. But that last word, sanctuary, makes it a specialty store kind of park. There's no playground, basketball court or soccer field at Corkscrew Swamp Sanctuary. Its main amenity is a fascinating 2.25-mile boardwalk that winds through six habitats in the sanctuary, where visitors may see more wildlife than at a zoo.

Corkscrew Swamp, which was designated as a National Natural Landmark in 1964, contains the largest old growth Bald Cypress forest in North America, according to the National Audubon Society. The well-maintained boardwalk leads visitors to 12 landmark cypress trees, which includes information about each. Examples: Landmark Tree No. 2 is more than 500 years old; Landmark Tree No. 3 is 22 feet around; and Landmark No. 10 is 104 feet tall. The trees are gorgeous reflections of our

Live Like A Tourist ... in in the Great Outdoors

region's history as some show hurricane damage while others are adorned with epiphytes such as the rare ghost orchid, which typically blooms in July or August. There are other, more common but equally beautiful, epiphytes scattered around the sanctuary as well.

The boardwalk leads guests through these six habitats where wildlife is everywhere: Lettuce Lakes, Central Marsh, Pond Cypress, Bald Cypress, Wet Prairie and Pine Flatwood. Informational signs are located throughout the boardwalk, providing interesting facts about trees and wildlife.

The sanctuary is home to 64 species of reptiles and amphibians, 34 mammals and 200 species of birds. The following is just a sampling of the wildlife observed: swallow-tailed kite, red-shouldered hawk (including a chick), alligators (including very young ones), anhinga (with chicks), roseate spoonbill, wood stork, raccoon (with its cubs), barred owl and various herons. It is the "best/coolest/most amazing park" for those interested in birding or nature photography.

There are volunteers along the boardwalk who may point out wildlife or offer additional information. There also may be scopes set up allowing visitors to get a close-up view of active nests.

There are benches along the boardwalk to rest. There is a lot of shade (some naturally provided by the canopy of trees and some offered by man-made shelters).

A shorter 1-mile boardwalk also is available for those who cannot traverse the full 2.25-mile boardwalk.

Inside the Blair Audubon Center, which is where you begin your adventure and pay your entry fee, is a theater, restroom and nature store, which offers a lot of good gifts and souvenirs. There, you also can pick up mosquito repellent if you forgot yours. For those less interested in wildlife, consider this a side trip to shopping at Coconut Point or at Miromar Outlets, both in Estero.

If You Go

Where: Corkscrew Swamp Sanctuary, 375 Sanctuary Road West, Estero

Tips: Wear mosquito repellent and comfortable shoes. Bring water, binoculars and a camera. If you are interested in the rare ghost orchid, call or check the websites in July to see if it is blooming.

Extra tip: Strollers and wheelchairs are available for free.

More info: 239-348-9151 or *http://corkscrew.audubon.org*

CREW (Corkscrew Regional Ecosystem Watershed), Southern Lee/Northern Collier counties

Some people will spend more than $50 for a white-noise machine that includes a bird-chirping option.

Or, you can take a recording device to the Bird Rookery Swamp Trail, which is part of the 60,000-acre Corkscrew Regional Ecosystem Watershed, also called CREW, in southern Lee and northern Collier counties.

The Bird Rookery Swamp Trail guides visitors along a boardwalk, then onto a grassy berm as you go deeper into the swamp. The berm/trail is unlike the boardwalk, where wildlife is less expected. Visitors should expect to see alligators lazily basking in the sun. Hikers also may hear and see river otters somersaulting beneath the surface of the water with the ease of synchronized swimmers. Panthers, bobcats and deer also have been spotted. And all of this takes place within a few feet of hikers while the birds noisily squawk and sing from above in the trees.

It is one of the most amazing true wildlife experiences in Southwest Florida.

CREW is composed of the following trail systems and includes the well-known National Audubon's Corkscrew Swamp Sanctuary: Bird Rookery Swamp, Corkscrew Marsh and Cypress Dome. Flint Pen Strand and Camp Keais Strand also make up CREW, which was "established in 1989 as a nonprofit organization to coordinate the land acquisition, land management, and public use," states the website, www.crewtrust.org. CREW works "with the South Florida Water Management District (which owns and manages the land) and the Florida Fish & Wildlife Conservation Commission (which monitors wildlife, hunting, and provides law enforcement on CREW)."

If you have time for only one of the trails, go to the Bird Rookery Swamp, 1295 Shady Hollow Blvd., Naples.

From the parking lot, follow the quarter-mile shell trail that leads to the 1,800-foot boardwalk, which is the beginning of the 12-mile trail.

Live Like A Tourist ... in in the Great Outdoors

"The trails are actually old tram roads used when the area was logged many years ago," states the website. "Biking can be a challenge on the grassy/sandy trails, but quite rewarding."

Because most of the trail is on the berm, wild animals may cross your path or share the berm. During my visit, a cottonmouth snake joined me on the trail. The head and about 3 inches of its body were actually on the trail, while the rest of him was hidden in taller grass. Had I been walking close to that edge, I might have stepped on him.

"Cottonmouths are semi-aquatic and can be found near water and fields," according to the Smithsonian National Zoo. "They inhabit brackish waters and are commonly found in swamps, streams, marshes, and drainage ditches in the southern lowlands of the United States."

If You Go

Where: 60,000-acre Corkscrew Regional Ecosystem Watershed. Go to the website to pick the trail system you want to visit.
More info: 239-657-2253 or *www.crewtrust.org*
Tips: Wear comfortable walking/hiking shoes, bring water and binoculars/camera.

Cottonmouths have very few predators, and therefore they are not threatened or endangered.

"Humans are wary of these venomous snakes and try to kill them, but nonvenomous water snakes are often mistaken for cottonmouths," states the Smithsonian National Zoo's website. "As a result, more non-venomous water snakes are killed every year than cottonmouths."

Aside from the snake, river otters and alligators, the bird activity is quite prevalent and noisy. Sometimes it's easier to spot the birds when you close your eyes and let your ears guide you.

Visitors don't have to walk or bike the entire 12 miles. Most walked in for a mile or two, turned around and walked back to their cars. Note: There is no water source for drinking nor are there bathrooms.

CREW Marsh Trails, 4600 CR 850 (Corkscrew Road), Immokalee, provides six miles of trails. The unique features here are the boardwalks and an observation tower. The trails are well-marked. Again, bring water.

Cypress Dome Trails, 3980 CR 850 (Corkscrew Road), Immokalee, opened in 2008. It was the least populated of the trail systems during my visits. Florida Gulf Coast University students helped number markers for self-guided tours along the six miles of trails.

Bird Rookery Swamp, CREW Marsha and Cypress Dome trails are great for birders, wildlife photographers, hikers, bikers and geocachers (check the website for the coordinates before you go).

Fakahatchee Strand Preserve State Park, Collier County

When loved ones visit, especially these who live north of the Mason-Dixon, they have expectations about their trip to Florida.

Some want to feel the sugary sand between their toes. Some want to reel in a tasty redfish. Some want to sink a putt in 75-degree weather… in February.

Many, I might even say most, want to see wildlife they don't see in their Michigan/Massachusetts/New York parks: manatees, dolphins, alligators.

You could take them to some roadside, sewage-smelling box on the outskirts

of the Everglades, where your guests will see those dangerous-looking alligators trapped in spaces smaller than some backyards. Your loved one may even be able to hold a small alligator, which may or may not have its mouth taped. Good luck with that.

Or, you could take them to see wildlife in the actual wild… you know, where the alligators actually swim in water and soak in the sun on the land.

So skip those animal freak shows and take your loved ones to one of the many wildlife refuges or state parks in Southwest Florida.

Good options for wildlife viewing include: J.N. "Ding" Darling National Wildlife Refuge on Sanibel Island, Bird Rookery Swamp Trail and Corkscrew Swamp Sanctuary near Naples, Six Mile Cypress Slough Preserve near Fort Myers and Myakka River State Park in Sarasota County. Here's another one to add to your list: Fakahatchee Strand Preserve State Park in Collier County.

Fakahatchee tends to be overlooked by the big national parks to the east and northwest: Everglades and Ding Darling. But there it is in Collier County, with its funny sounding name, occupying a 20-mile long strip of land that is also 5 miles wide.

Live Like A Tourist ... **in in the Great Outdoors**

"Its groves of native royal palms are the most abundant in the state, and the ecosystem of the Fakahatchee Strand is the only place in the world where bald cypress trees and royal palms share the forest canopy," according to the Florida State Parks' website. "It is the orchid and bromeliad capital of the continent with 44 native orchids and 14 native bromeliad species."

Fakahatchee is known for its orchids, and especially the ghost orchid. Thieves have been known to steal these elusive orchids, which became the subject of Susan Orlean's "The Orchid Thief," and later the film, "Adaptation."

If You Go

Where: Fakahatchee Strand Preserve State Park, 137 Coastline Drive, Copeland
Tips: Wear mosquito repellent and don't stand beneath a wood stork.
More info: 239-695-4593 or *www.floridastateparks.org/park/ Fakahatchee-Strand*

"Habitat destruction and hydrologic changes due to human development in South Florida have been partially responsible for the decline of ghost orchid populations," according to the National Park Service. "Also, over-collecting has had a negative impact on this special plant."

The endangered and protected ghost orchid only blooms (if it blooms) in the middle of summer.

There are two sections to Fakahatchee: The large park area where there are long trails for serious hikers and even a scenic drive for those who don't want to walk. Then there's the Big Cypress Bend Boardwalk, which is perfect for those looking to see a lot of wildlife in a concentrated area (or for those who get lost easily).

The 2,500-foot boardwalk provides informational signs about the park's beautiful trees, plants and wildlife.

The boardwalk ends in a swamp, which probably looks like what our northern loved ones expect to see in South Florida: alligators, a cottonmouth snake, endangered wood storks, herons, egrets and river otters. It's a postcard. It's a scene for a jigsaw puzzle. It's beautiful, and it's real Florida.

Take your loved ones to local, state and county parks, where your guests can experience real Florida wildlife.

Fort DeSoto Park, Tierra Verde

Dr. Beach, you got it right.

Fort DeSoto Park in Pinellas County is one of the best beaches I've experienced. Dr. Beach rated it the No. 1 Beach in America in 2005. TripAdvisor named it America's Top Beach in 2009.

"We love this beach. It's always our favorite place to go when we're down on vacation. They're always doing work to improve upon the park. Very clean park with shower houses and snack bar. You can also find more secluded beach areas on the park grounds," a reviewer wrote on TripAdvisor.

More than 2.7 million people annually visit Fort DeSoto Park, according to Pinellas County officials. Don't let that scare you away. There is still plenty of room for umbrellas, chairs, towels, and even a little football tossing since the park consists of 1,136 acres, five interconnected islands, 7 miles of waterfront and almost 3 miles of soft, sugar-doughnut sand beach.

Snowbirds go back north because it's "hot" down here in the summer. OK, sure, it's warm. But guess what? So is the water. The bathtub-like Gulf temperatures and the white powdery beaches are ideal in the summer, and Fort DeSoto Park definitely tops the list.

Fort DeSoto Park is different from many others due to its history, beauty, clear Gulf water and varied amenities.

Let's start with the most unique one, the fort's Battery Laidley, which also is what distinguishes it from other Gulf beaches.

Pinellas County's website offers a 24-page history of the Fort and islands, which first were inhabited by the Tocobaga Indians. The property belonged to the federal government at times.

"Fort DeSoto was never the site of any major battle," the county's website states. "In fact, the weapons of forts DeSoto and Dade were never fired in combat. However that era was significant in terms of the evolution of modern weaponry."

The U.S. sold the property back to Pinellas County after World War II.

"Extensive plans were drawn up and many dreams became a reality on May 11, 1963, when Fort DeSoto Park was officially

Live Like A Tourist ... **in in the Great Outdoors**

dedicated," the county's website states. "In 1977, the Fort DeSoto batteries were placed on the National Register of Historic Places."

The 24-page brochure online includes information for the self-guided tour, which is "home to the last four surviving carriage-mounted 12-inch seacoast mortars in the continental United States," the website states. Print self-guided tour information before you go. There were no fliers available when I visited the park.

Fort DeSoto Park easily is a full day of fun. One could spend several days there, and the park offers 238 campsites for just that reason.

You can start the day fishing on one of the two piers, and bait is sold at the piers as well.

For those who don't care for fishing (you can't blame a girl for not wanting to touch the bait or fish), there are hiking and biking trails throughout the park. Don't worry about bringing a bicycle, as you can rent one for a reasonable fee.

Those who would rather be on the water can launch their own kayaks/canoes, or rent them.

At some point during your adventure, hop on the ferry to Egmont Key National Wildlife Refuge, which once was the site of Fort Dade.

If you are just looking for a place to lounge on the beach, head to North Beach. It's a popular spot, and probably the most beautiful spot to take a nap on the soft sand. It's also near the shorebird habitat area, which is protected for the nesting birds. Wildlife is very abundant at Fort DeSoto, so birders would have a great time too.

If You Go

Where: Fort DeSoto Park, 3500 Pinellas Bayway S., Tierra Verde
More info: 727-582-2267 or *www.pinellascounty.org/park/05_ft_desoto.htm*

There are plenty of picnic shelters. In addition, there are concessions if you forget to pack a cooler of goodies.

Those who can't part with their furry kids can take them as well. They even have their own dog beach.

Dr. Beach's 2015 list of top 10 beaches included these Florida parks: Barefoot Beach, Bonita Springs (No. 2); St. George Island State Park, Florida panhandle (No. 3); Cape Florida State Park, Key Biscayne (No. 6); and Delnor-Wiggins Pass State Park, Naples (No. 9).

Skip Barefoot Beach and Delnor-Wiggins, and drive north to Fort DeSoto… until Dr. Beach finally comes around and puts Englewood's Stump Pass Beach State Park on his list.

We're waiting, Dr. Beach.

Four Mile Cove Ecological Preserve, Cape Coral

Cape Coral offers a unique two-for-one attraction near the base of the Midpoint Bridge, where motorists can quickly spot the most recognizable feature: the 20-foot Iwo Jima statue.

The 40-year-old monument is located in the Veterans Memorial Area, which is in the 365-acre Four Mile Cove Ecological Preserve (also known as Eco Park to locals).

The Iwo Jima statue is one of three replicas by sculptor Felix de Weldon, who created the original 60-foot U.S. Marine Corps War Memorial near the Arlington National Cemetery in Virginia, according to the Southwest Florida Military Museum and Library. The statue was inspired by the famous, Pulitzer Prize-winning photograph by Joe Rosenthal of The Associated Press.

Interestingly, the Cape Coral replica wasn't always located in Eco Park. In 1964, Gulf American Corporation had the statue built for the Cape's first tourist attraction, The Rose Garden. For those who weren't in Southwest Florida in the 1960s, which is most of us, imagine a place that symbolizes what Florida really is… a hodgepodge of the ordinary mixed with a side of nuttiness. The Rose Garden — part-Bellagio-like with its Waltzing Waters fountain show, part-SeaWorld with porpoise shows, part-botanical gardens, part-zoo — closed in 1970.

Live Like A Tourist ... in in the Great Outdoors

"The statue remained in the Rose Gardens long after it was abandoned and overgrown," wrote Jeff Koehn on *www.capecoral.com*. "In the early 1980s, Cape Coral bank official Mike Geml stumbled upon a pile of concrete and stones and soon realized he had found the memorial, which had suffered years of neglect and vandalism. Geml made it a personal mission to restore the statue and in 1980 moved the statue to the then-North First Bank located on Del Prado Boulevard near Viscaya Parkway. Geml spent the next year raising funds and awareness to have the statue restored. During that time, de Weldon made a trip to Cape Coral to see the condition of the statue and was so overwhelmed by its disrepair, that he sent two of his people to Cape Coral to repair and restore the statue."

In 1998, the statue was moved to Eco Park, where it was designated as a Florida Historical Site.

In addition to the Iwo Jima statue, there are other monuments in the Veterans Memorial Area that honor the men and women who have served during various wars.

The second attraction is Eco Park itself, which includes a small visitors center and a 6,600-foot walking trail that winds through mangroves. There are informational signs along the way, offering details about the area's fauna and flora.

If You Go

Where: Four Mile Cove Ecological Preserve, East end of Southeast 23rd Terrace, Cape Coral
Cost: Donations accepted
Tips: Wear comfortable shoes and take mosquito repellent
More info on the park:
www.capecoral.net/department/ parks_and_recreationhome/ four_mile_cove_eco_preserve. php

The boardwalk eventually leads to two separate piers overlooking the Caloosahatchee River, where visitors can soak in some sun on a bench or watch birds.

Live Like A Tourist ... **in the Great Outdoors**

Garden of the Five Senses, North Port

It was one of those summer mornings… as if God bit into an orange, misting the sweet, sticky juice on South Florida.

It was breezeless. Still. Heavy with that heavenly humidity.

Yet somehow the leaves slowly fanned themselves and the flower petals slightly quivered in a wind that wasn't there.

Thousands of bees, along with a few butterflies, breathed life into the garden that day. Their nonstop buzzing and fluttering made one believe that a 10 mph wind constantly blew despite the beads of sweat-necklaces forming beneath the beating sun.

That's the beauty of the Garden of the Five Senses in North Port. It truly taps into your senses.

"The concept for the park was first brought to the city by the late Jean Bruhn, who visited a similar park in Lancaster, Pa. At the time, Bruhn was a member of the city's Parks and Recreation Advisory Board. She envisioned a park that would be easily accessible to the disabled and maintained by the community," according to Erin Bryce, community outreach manager for the city of North Port, in 2007 when the park opened. "Already, the community has contributed to the Garden. People for Trees and members of the Cub Scout Pack and Boy Scout Troop No. 257 hosted a tree-planting and dedication in mid-October. The organizations planted two sweet gums, which are fast-growing, native Florida shade trees."

"The Garden of the Five Senses, located on Pan American Drive just south of the Jockey Club, is designed to entice each of the five senses amid a garden of Florida landscape," Bryce wrote.

Sight is the most obvious of the senses used in the garden, which makes up 3.5 acres in a 16.1-acre park.

Live Like A Tourist ... **in in the Great Outdoors**

Where: Garden of the Five
Senses, 4299 Pan American
Blvd., North Port
More info: 941-429-PARK or
*www.cityofnorthport.com/
city-hall/parks-recreation/
parks/garden-of-the-five-senses*

The garden is broken up into different areas such as a wildlife, oasis garden or succulent garden. Standing still in each area is how one can see the smallest of the garden's residents. Literally, thousands of bees fly in and out of flowers. They don't mind you watching. In fact, not one bee came near me (but for those with bee allergies, I suppose it would be a good idea to keep that EpiPen on hand just in case the bully bee strikes).

Birds, including a brilliant blue jay, can be spotted as well.

The park also features a life-size sundial, which instructs you where to stand based on the month and to raise your hand. Your shadow will reveal the time (and it worked for me).

Sound can be difficult to appreciate in parks — especially smaller ones or those near roadways. Again, just as with vision, one needs stillness. The best place in the garden to appreciate sound is in the Zen Garden section, where a small waterfall drowns out human-made noises. The peaceful trickling of water adds to the tranquility of the park.

Again, the best way to appreciate this sense is by stillness so you can hear the birds and the rustling of leaves.

Smells can be found through a variety of plants and flowers. Sniff away.

Touching can be accomplished in various ways. One can sit beside the statue "Brother Reading Book," and read a book alongside him. Sweet gum trees help keep visitors cool by providing shade as well.

Taste… this is where it gets a little tricky. I'm not sure I tasted anything physically. Perhaps if you bring a picnic lunch, then the fifth sense could be experienced. Or if you get stuck in a rain shower, tilt your head back, open your mouth and taste the droplets. But aside from that, I don't recommend going around trying to eat the plants… or the wildlife. That's normally frowned upon in a public park.

Taste aside, the Garden of the Five (Four) Senses is a special park — one the citizens of North Port can enjoy now and even more later after future improvements.

Highlands Hammock State Park, Sebring

Some parks are known for beauty, amenities or wildlife. Highlands Hammock State Park has all of that plus a fascinating history.

Like Myakka River State Park, Highlands Hammock's roots can be traced back to the Civil Conservation Corps — President Franklin Roosevelt's program that helped employ 3 million young men who worked in parks and forests, according to PBS.

"After planting 3 billion trees in nine years of service, the CCC dissolved in July of 1942," states the introduction to PBS' piece called, "The Civil Conservation Corps." "As the economy began to improve in the late 1930s, young men found higher-paying jobs at home, and the number of CCC camps across the country dwindled. President Roosevelt's attempt at turning it into a permanent agency failed. After the bombing of Pearl Harbor and subsequent U.S. involvement in World War II, the CCC's funding and assets were diverted as the nation's focus shifted toward the war effort. The legacy of the CCC continues to live on in the hundreds of campgrounds, hiking trails and swimming holes still enjoyed by Americans today."

A museum dedicated to the CCC in Florida is located at Highlands Hammock, which the CCC operated from 1933 to 1936. The building itself was built by the CCC.

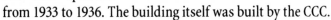

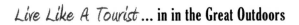

"During nine years in Florida, close to 50,000 young men from poverty-stricken families were given wholesome employment and their families were paid $25 per month, which permitted them to live through the worst depression that our nation has ever endured," states an exhibit at the museum.

Highlands Hammock occupies more than 9,000 acres of wildlife-filled trails and campsites, but it isn't too large for most to enjoy. Like at Myakka River State Park, visitors can drive to most trailheads — cutting down on the steps for those who can't walk long distances.

If You Go

Where: Highlands Hammock State Park, 5931 Hammock Road, Sebring
More info: 863-386-6094 or *www.floridastateparks.org/park/ Highlands-Hammock*
Tips: Wear good walking shoes and mosquito repellent; take drinking water. Take a picnic lunch or plan to eat in Sebring or another nearby town.

There are nine well-marked trails ranging from 975 feet to 3,005 feet. There also is the 3.1-mile Loop Drive, which can be enjoyed by bicyclists as well.

There are three must-do, 20-30-minute trails:

- Richard Lieber Memorial Trail — The 1,791-foot trail begins with the 1,000-year-old live oak, which is considered the "oldest living thing in the Hammock," states the brochure.
- Cypress Swamp Trail —This 2,355-foot trail is amazing with its historic catwalks in addition to boardwalks. Those who have balance issues may not want to cross the narrow catwalks that carry visitors over swampy, gator-infested water.
- Fern Garden Trail — The 1,641-foot trail "takes you through a hardwood swamp area, where you are very likely to spot alligators," states the brochure. This is true, and I saw a very large gator within a few feet of the trail.

A tram ride also is available around the park for an additional fee.

"The tram is fully accessible and allows those who cannot, or choose not to walk, to see the park and observe wildlife," states the park's website.

This is a full-day adventure, but definitely take your own picnic lunch or plan to eat somewhere in Sebring.

Historic Spanish Point, Osprey

So much of life is a series of accidents and happenstance.

Had John Webb not run into a Spanish trader in Key West, it's likely Historic Spanish Point would be known by a different name.

Had Bertha Palmer not settled in Sarasota County, it's likely Historic Spanish Point wouldn't be the preserved historical site it is today.

Historic Spanish Point is a "30-acre environmental, archaeological, and historical site," states its website. I would add a few more words so it reads: "A beautiful, impeccably landscaped, 30-acre environmental, archaeological, and historical site on peaceful Little Sarasota Bay."

Historic Spanish Point's history can be broken down into four chapters.

First chapter: The Prehistory era

There are locations around Southwest Florida where middens (like an old garbage pile or landfill) have been found and excavated. "Prehistoric people living on our bay's shore saw the introduction of ceramics and the transition from nomadic hunters and gatherers to settled subsistence societies," states its website. "They capitalized on the abundant resources provided by the gulf, marsh, woodland and bay ecosystems and utilized growing specialized tool technology to further establish the permanent and seasonal settlements."

"A Window to the Past" exhibition provides visitors with a unique opportunity to see into a shell midden through glass walls. "This is the only exhibition in the world where you can be surrounded by a prehistoric shell mound," states its website. This is a must-see stop during your trip to Historic Spanish Point.

Second chapter: The Webbs

For some reason, the prehistoric residents abandoned Historic Spanish Point sometime before 1100. Scientists believe the property remained uninhabited until the Webbs came along in 1867. The Webbs flourished in Florida, planting citrus, vegetables

Live Like A Tourist ... in in the Great Outdoors

and sugar cane. They encouraged others to spend the winters in Florida, and thus the Webbs' Winter Resort became the first of its kind in the region. Most of the Webbs are buried on the property in the Pioneer Cemetery.

Third chapter: Bertha Palmer

In 1910, Chicago socialite Bertha Palmer came to Florida looking for a winter home.

"She came down here with her $8 million and bought up a good portion of South Sarasota County," said volunteer docent Sue Anders.

Part of the land she acquired included Webb's, where she maintained the buildings and linked them with gardens. She was active in cattle ranching and her 15,000-acre Meadowsweet Pastures later became part of the Myakka River State Park.

Palmer died in 1918. Her family maintained the property, which she called Osprey Point. Her grandson, Gordon, "sponsored the three-year excavation by Ripley P. Bullen of the archaeological site which now encompasses the museum at Historic Spanish Point," states the website.

Relatives understood its historical significance, and in 1976, "it became the first site in Sarasota County to be listed in the National Register of Historic Places," states the website. The Palmer relatives donated the property in 1980 to the Gulf Coast Heritage Association, which operates Historic Spanish Point today.

Fourth chapter: Today

Because of the prehistoric residents, the Webbs and the Palmers, visitors today can stroll the gorgeous grounds and learn about the past at Historic Spanish Point.

In addition to "A Window to the Past," visitors also should make it a point to stop by Mary's Chapel, which originally was built by John Webb's son. It was rebuilt in 1986, using the chapel's original stained-glass windows.

"It's very popular today for small weddings," Sue said.

Palmer's Sunken Garden and Pergola also is a well-known site for weddings.

There's too much history and too many interesting stories to learn (Why was the chapel named after a girl named Mary? Why is there a long boardwalk? Why are there so many blue-colored flowers?), so be sure to set aside a few hours to explore Historic Spanish Point.

Live Like A Tourist ... **in the Great Outdoors**

History Park, Punta Gorda

There's a lot of history all around Punta Gorda.

But on a few acres of land fertilized with passion and preservation, History Park has grown into a destination that attracts thousands each week.

The Price House, built in 1914, moved to History Park in 2004. The original owner's influence remains in Punta Gorda today. Maxwell Charles Price, who worked as a city engineer, city manager and mayor, designed the First United Methodist Church of Punta Gorda, according to an informational pamphlet provided at the park.

The newest addition to the History Park, the Quednau/Hindman House, 1925, is being renovated.

The first stage is creating an office space in the L-shaped porch of the 1924 home. The second, more exciting stage involves re-establishing a children's museum in the 3,400-square-foot house.

It's strange for me to see the Quednau/Hindman House anywhere but across from my old apartment on Goldstein Street, where the county's first Supervisor

of Elections Tosie Hindman lived for many years. While I knew about Tosie, I didn't know much about her father, Fred Quednau, who worked as a "commercial fisherman, a cafe owner, Punta Gorda Mayor and County Sheriff," states the informational pamphlet. Quednau served as sheriff for 16 years, and had a force of a whopping two deputies, according to the Sheriff's Office.

Starr Zachritz, who runs the art gallery and provides garden tours, works out of the oldest building in the park. The History Park Art Gallery and Gift Shop, which is a great place for one-of-a-kind gifts and souvenirs, is located in the 1885 Trabue Land Sales Office.

"I feel proud to be in the oldest building in the park," Starr said.

The building, the oldest in Charlotte County, once served as a post office.

The fourth building in the park is the Cigar Cottage, which became the first structure in the park on Oct. 12, 1999.

Volunteers do all renovations on the buildings, as well as the landscaping and gardening in the park.

A farmers market brings in 1,500 to 2,000 people on Sundays. Visitors can shop for fruits, plants, purses, candles, teas, jewelry and more.

Weddings, parties and reunions can be scheduled at the History Park, where beautiful lights hang from trees. Fees from events and vendors help pay for the park's bills.

If You Go

Where: Punta Gorda History Park, 501 Shreve St.
More info: *http:// puntagordahistory.com/ ourhistoricbuildings/ thehistorypark.html*

J.N. "Ding" Darling National Wildlife Refuge, Sanibel Island

I first heard about the J.N. "Ding" Darling National Wildlife Refuge during the closing nature segment on the "CBS Sunday Morning" show.

You know this segment. This is the one in which Charles Osgood says, "We now leave you at... (some beautiful, amazing place where there's water rippling, birds chirping and deer looking surprised because that's how deer look)." Then you get off your couch and think, "That looks cool. I should go there sometime."

And then you don't.

And then the years pass.

Finally, I got off the couch and made it to Ding Darling on Sanibel Island.

Now I know why CBS profiled the wildlife refuge. It's beautiful. But it's more than that. It's a sliver of land in this great big world we actually protected from ourselves.

The J.N. "Ding" Darling National Wildlife Refuge is the largest wildlife refuge in a complex that totals about 8,000 acres in Southwest Florida.

According to park information, Ding Darling is the home to:

- 30-plus kinds of mammals.
- 102 species of fish.
- 14 threatened or endangered animals, some of which include eastern indigo snakes, American crocodiles, alligators, wood storks, manatees, several kinds of sea turtles, smalltooth sawfish and piping plovers.
- 272 species of birds.
- 60 kinds of reptiles and amphibians (for the record, I only saw turtles and alligators... thank goodness).

More than 750,000 people visit Ding Darling each year, such as Eileen and Ed Michaels of Columbia, S.C. They chose to spend the last day of their Sanibel Island vacation at Ding Darling.

Live Like A Tourist ... **in in the Great Outdoors**

"It's very well done," Eileen said.

The wildlife refuge's main attraction is Wildlife Drive, a four-mile path that can be viewed by foot, bicycle or vehicle.

You will be provided a map that highlights certain areas of the drive, such as the Calusa Shell Mound Trail along with good places for bird/wildlife watching. The great thing about the drive is that you can stop anywhere along the way. Simply pull your vehicle to the right, park and get out of the car. The Wildlife Drive is one way for vehicles and bicycles so don't try turning around or driving in reverse. Planning note: Do not go on Fridays. The Wildlife Drive is closed this one day of the week for maintenance, research, etc.

If You Go

Where: J.N. "Ding" Darling National Wildlife Refuge, 1 Wildlife Drive, Sanibel Island
More info: 239-472-1100 or *http://www.fws.gov/dingdarling*
Tips: Rent or bring bicycles to explore the Wildlife Drive (it's better than driving). It is also recommended to visit from December to March, when the birding is best. Bring binoculars and a camera as well.

Along Wildlife Drive, expect to see many species of birds, especially at low tide. It's truly a bird-watcher's paradise.

Ding Darling's website includes an "eBird Trail Tracker," which provides daily counts of the kinds of birds spotted in the refuge: *http://www.fws.gov/dingdarling/eBird.html.*

For those who prefer the view from the water, there are two kayak/canoe launches along the drive. Fishing is allowed in some areas. Go to *www.fws.gov/southeast/pubs/Ding-Darling-fish-broch.pdf* to read the rules and regulations for fishing and boating.

There's something for everyone at Ding Darling, including a very interesting Visitor/Education Center. There, guests can learn about the wildlife refuge's namesake (who happened to be a Pulitzer Prize-winning cartoonist) and inhabitants.

Carve out a full day for Ding Darling in order to give yourself enough time to enjoy the wildlife refuge, and also to spend some time at the education center and gift shop, which is a great place to pick up some holiday gifts while supporting Ding Darling.

This needs to be high on your local bucket list — especially if you want to see the white pelicans that will migrate to Florida (keep an eye on the ebird Trail Tracker). You will leave Ding Darling as relaxed as you are watching the CBS "Sunday Morning" segment from the comfort of your couch.

Koreshan State Historic Site, Estero

It turns out Florida has been quirky for quite a long time.

In the late 1800s, a man named Cyrus Reed Teed took his Koreshanity followers to Estero, where he planned to create the New Jerusalem for 10 million people. It was described as "Utopia… a life without crime, tobacco or drugs," states the brochure for self-guided tours at the Koreshan State Historic Site.

Sounds lovely, right?

"The Koreshan Unity was founded upon the ideas of communal living and property, the belief in Dr. Teed's religious and scientific theories, and the communistic goal of everyone working for the good of all," the brochure states.

Sounds a little like summer camp…

The Koreshans believed "the universe existed on the inside of the Earth," states one of the landmarks at the park.

Sounds… wait, inside what?

The Koreshan Unity members lived on about 300 acres of land in Estero in Lee County, which is now a state park and historic site dedicated to preserving their history and the beautiful land.

"A major tenet of Koreshan belief was the theory of 'cellular cosmogony' — living inside the Earth. Teed reasoned that God would not create an infinite universe, for the infinite is beyond the reach of human understanding and man could not comprehend it," an informational sign at the park states. "In 1870, Teed claimed to have discovered that the Earth was a hollow sphere with all life contained in it. He said that the sun, moon, planets and stars were just an illusion, as they are, actually reflected up from the surface. Day and night were thought to be caused by a rotating ball of gases, at the center, sending a positive charge down from the light side

Live Like A Tourist … in in the Great Outdoors

and reflecting a negative charge back to the dark side. This acted like an electric motor and kept the day and night cycle spinning."

OK...

The Koreshans built numerous buildings that included a machine shop, houses, cottages and the beautiful Planetary Court, where the seven female members of the Planetary Court resided.

They also turned a wild Florida landscape into beautiful gardens and orchards.

"The gardens are described in the 1902 settlement plans as planted with many fruit and nut trees and other kinds of plants, which allude to biblical descriptions of Eden," the brochure states.

Epiphytes, or air plants, can be seen all over the Koreshan State Historic Site.

Most of the Koreshans came from Illinois, where the soil, of course, is quite different from here in tropical Southwest Florida.

"They learned from their neighbors and soon found success with a variety of vegetables, mainly tomatoes, cow peas, sweet potatoes, greens and beans," the brochure states. "Some vegetables were grown commercially and shipped, but the farming and gardening were the mainstays of the Koreshan tables."

If You Go

Where: Koreshan State Historic Site, 3800 Corkscrew Road, Estero

Tips: Wear comfortable shoes and mosquito repellent. Take drinking water. Also, take a little extra money (or more for a donation) to buy the self-guided tour brochure.

More info:
www.floridastateparks.org/ hours-and-fees/Koreshan

Teed died in 1908, and membership began to decline.

The Koreshan Unity lasted longer than one might expect (given how airplanes began flying around... inside the Earth; and Sputnik went into space... inside the Earth as well).

In 1961, the few remaining members gave the property to the state, which became the Koreshan State Historic Site, and is listed on the National Register of Historic Places.

Lakes Regional Park, Fort Myers

Two water features. Two large, multisensory playgrounds. Two-plus miles of trails. Botanic garden. Train rides. Bike rides. Pedal boat rides. Oh, and there's ice cream, too.

Lakes Regional Park, located south of Fort Myers, is an incredible, amenity-filled county-run facility. Families could spend an entire day at the 279-acre park. Or, it could serve as a great place to tire out little ones while shopping in Lee County.

When you pull into Lakes Park (as it's called for short), there are two ways to go:

- Right: Takes you to Parking Lot 3, which leads to the botanic garden, Railroad Depot, train-themed playground, sand volleyball court, amphitheater, large open field area. This also is the closest parking lot for the Whistle Stop Ice Cream shop, where they serve burgers, hot dogs, nachos and ice cream.

Live Like A Tourist ... in in the Great Outdoors

- Left: Takes you to Parking Lots 1 and 2. This part of the park includes the two different water feature parks, and another large playground.

There is access to pavilions, restrooms (very clean), pedal boat and bicycle rentals and walking trails through all three parking lots.

The main walking trail is a one-mile loop around the park. The trail is smooth and wide enough for strollers, bicycles, wheelchairs, etc. The park also offers other trails as well. The American Heart Association designated it as an official "Start! Walking Path" park.

If You Go

Where: Lakes Regional Park, 7330 Gladiolus Drive, Fort Myers
More info on the park and pavilion rentals: *LeeParks@ leegov.com* or 239-533-7275
More info on boat/bike rentals: 239-332-2453
More info on the train rides: 239-267-1905
Tips: No pets, alcohol or motorized/electric vehicles allowed. If you are into birding, bring binoculars and a camera.

Those looking for a workout can do just that on the trail, but those looking for a little nature viewing may want to bring binoculars for bird watching as the trail crosses a lake and winds through trees.

For kids, the highlights have to be the water features and playgrounds.

The water features looked like a lot of fun, and all the kids seemed to be having a great time. I wanted to try it out, but I didn't want to seem like the creepy childless grownup frolicking around, splashing other people's children... most frown upon that kind of behavior.

Same goes for the playgrounds. It took a lot of restraint to stay off the rock-climbing wall. I will confess to testing out one of the musical features in the train-themed playground. ... I had to see how it worked.

Families can enjoy the wide-open fields, as well, that offer plenty of room for tossing footballs or kicking soccer balls.

Adults should make sure to stop by the botanic garden, which offers beautiful flowers and trees along with information. My favorite part was the Fragrance Garden, but the Succulent Garden also is interesting.

For more information about Lakes Park, go to *www.leeparks.org*, click on *Facilities*, scroll down to Parks and then find it alphabetically.

Lemon Bay Park and Environmental Center, Englewood

Lepidoptera is a term we may hear more about in the future.

It's not a disease, though it kind of sounds like one. It's nothing to fear, though some people do and that's called lepidopterophobia... because there's a phobia for everything.

In reality, lepidoptera needs protection... just like tigers and rhinos. But moths and butterflies — lepidoptera — don't get the same kind of attention as the big mammals, though the monarch butterfly, especially, is in need of attention. And every butterfly garden helps keep them alive for future generations.

I stumbled on one of the best butterfly gardens in the area, which is located at Lemon Bay Park and Environmental Center on the Sarasota County side of Englewood. Prior to exploring the park, go into the Environmental Center and take one of the butterfly pamphlets. The flier details the dozens of butterflies and moths that can be spotted in the park, and in the garden. And it's not an exaggeration.

Quietly enter the well-marked butterfly garden, and remain still. Within a few minutes, or less, the garden comes alive.

"The longer you linger, the more activity you will see," states the flier.

It's an amazing experience to stand there as various kinds of butterflies flutter around you. It's alarming to think there could be a day when these beautiful, colorful creatures no longer exist.

Experts have already seen a decline in the monarch from 1 billion to 60 million in just the last 20 years, according to the National Fish and Wildlife Foundation.

Live Like A Tourist ... in in the Great Outdoors

"Species we take for granted will struggle to find new niches. Entire communities may be lost. While people will certainly notice as the big cats vanish, the thousands, if not tens of thousands, of moths and butterflies likely to be lost will fly below the radar. They will become 'collateral damage' as stressed ecosystems and societies adapt," wrote John Shuey, of the Indiana Office of the Nature Conservancy, in his paper "An Essay to the Future" on The Lepidopterists' Society website.

The Washington Post reported even more alarming news about the monarch butterfly.

"Monarch butterflies that alight from Mexico and fly across the United States to Canada are being massacred. The U.S. Fish and Wildlife Service laid out a grim statistic in February: Nearly a billion have vanished since 1990 as farmers and homeowners sprayed herbicides on milkweed, a plant the colorful creatures use as a food source, a home and a nursery. ... Mexican scientists and American conservationists announced that the killing field has widened in the worst place possible — a monarch sanctuary. More than 52 acres of a haven where the butterflies hibernate over winter has been degraded, mostly by deforestation from illegal logging, with drought helping the decline, they said," wrote Darryl Fears in *The Washington Post*.

The milkweed plant is crucial to the monarch's survival, and it can be planted anywhere.

"The butterfly habitat includes the garden and surrounding grassy meadow and woodlands," states the Lemon Bay Park pamphlet. "Specific plants have been planted to attract the butterfly species that live in this area."

Lemon Bay Park is 210 acres with 1.7 miles of shoreline along the Lemon Bay Aquatic Preserve.

In addition to the butterfly garden, the park offers well-maintained nature trails, picnicking areas and a kayak-canoe launch.

This isn't an all-day adventure, unless you plan to kayak/canoe, but it is a great place to lower the blood pressure, add a few steps to your pedometer and appreciate the butterflies.

Manatee Park, Fort Myers

Many of us never saw a manatee until we moved down here.

We never walked on a beach or dock "up north" and saw a little, whiskered snout surface for a breath of air. We never saw giant baked potato-like blobs slowly (really slowly) lumber through the water.

Now we can as Floridians, though sometimes they can be hard to find.

Winter is the ideal time of the year, however, to see manatees. And the best place to see dozens of them is at Manatee Park in Fort Myers, where manatees flock during the winter months. The Florida Power & Light facility discharges warm water into a canal that meets with the Orange River, providing manatees with a warm environment when the Gulf of Mexico dips below 68 degrees.

The large number of manatees frolicking in slow-mo attracted a lot of attention. Therefore, in 1996, Lee County and FPL created the 17-acre park so guests could view the manatees in a noncaptive refuge. Visitors also can learn a lot about manatees from the informational signs around the park, as well as through the lectures provided at various times.

Live Like A Tourist ... in in the Great Outdoors

The park is very easy to find: On Palm Beach Boulevard (State Road 80) just east of Interstate 75 in Fort Myers. More than 150,000 people visit Manatee Park each year, according to Lee County.

There are two ways to view the manatees: by land and by sea.

Most people see the manatees from the numerous viewing areas on land in the park. There is a pier/boardwalk along with a long stretch of sidewalk that winds along the canal, where many of the manatees are visible swimming near the surface and delighting visitors with the familiar sounds of their puffy exhales. There are several observation areas, including one lagoon-like area where there is a special speaker that allows guests to listen to the manatees communicate underwater.

The second way to see the manatees is via kayak or canoe. Manatees literally surface right next to kayaks and canoes, sometimes even nosing the vessels. Definitely bring a camera if you go out on the water.

You can bring your own kayak/canoe to the park, or you can rent one.

There is a small gift shop with manatee postcards, ornaments, T-shirts, photos and other manatee-related gifts. And if the little ones need to get rid of some more energy before leaving Manatee Park, there is a playground as well.

Speaking of little ones, if you plan to take them, go online to the Lee County's website for Manatee Park: *https://www.leegov.com/parks/facility?fid=00880088*. There, you can find a 10-page Manatee Activity Book that you can print at home. It includes pictures to color, a word puzzle, facts about manatees and other activities. There's also Manatee Park Bingo, which can be a fun way for kids to unknowingly learn while at the park.

If You Go

Where: Manatee Park, 10901 Palm Beach Blvd. (State Road 80), Fort Myers
Tips: Go in the winter, and especially before the end of March.
More info: 239-690-5030
More info on renting kayaks/ canoes: 239-481-4600

Marie Selby Botanical Gardens, Sarasota

Orchid lovers, plant lovers, flower lovers and peace lovers will love Marie Selby Botanical Gardens in Sarasota. (That's a lot of love, but it's true.)

Selby Gardens sits on 14-plus acres overlooking Sarasota Bay and the Hudson Bayou. William and Marie Selby bought seven acres on the bay and built a two-story home there in the early 1920s. William died in 1956, followed by Marie in 1971.

"The contents of Marie Selby's will revealed her wish to leave her property to the community as a botanical garden 'for the enjoyment of the general public,'" according to *www.selby.org*. "A board of directors was appointed, and after consultation with the New York Botanical Garden and the University of Florida, it was decided that the garden should specialize in epiphytic plants, thereby making it unique among the more than 200 botanical gardens in the country."

Epiphytic plants sometimes are referred to as "air plants." They grow on other plants (but not like a non-rent-paying roommate who mooches off you). Epiphytes aren't parasitic. You've probably seen them but had no idea you were looking at something called epiphytes. Example: Spanish moss.

"Florida has the richest epiphyte flora in the United States," according to *www.selby.org*. "Of the approximately 85 native epiphytic ferns and flowering plants, nearly two-thirds are found in Florida only in swamps of the Fakahatchee Strand State Preserve and Big Cypress National Preserve, and tropical hammocks of Everglades National Park." (In case you were wondering — I was — where Fakahatchee

Live Like A Tourist ... in in the Great Outdoors

Where: Marie Selby Botanical Gardens, 900 South Palm Ave., Sarasota

More info: *www.selby.org* or 941-366-5731

Strand State Preserve is located, it's just west of Big Cypress in South Florida.)

Selby Gardens opened in 1975 and eventually expanded to today's current size.

The first stop on your tour of Selby Gardens likely will be the Conservatory, which is a rainforest-like setting filled with beautiful, colorful orchids and bromeliads along with other kinds of epiphytes. Each is numbered with an interesting description provided on a "Gems of the Rainforest 2013 Plant List," which conveniently is located on the back side of a map of the gardens. There are 16 "gems" described on the sheet (it can be like a fun scavenger hunt to locate all of them).

The next stops include the Sho Fu Bonsai Exhibit and Conservatory Patio, Cycad Display, followed by the Banyan Grove, where I lost track of time taking photos. The Grove houses the original fig trees planted by the Selbys in the 1930s. Guests can walk beneath the trees that arc above the walkway.

Continue along the path toward the Schimmel Wedding Lawn and Pavilion and take a seat on a bench where the bayou and the bay meet. You can spend a lot of time fantasizing about the mansions and looking for dolphins while various seabirds dive for lunch. After resting the legs, stroll down the Mangroves and Baywalk path marked on the map. Look closely as the trees and plants provide flora-framed photographs of sailboats in the bay.

Tea lovers can stop in the Carriage House, where samples are offered. Selby does offer a restaurant (located inside the Selbys' house) that serves sandwiches and salads.

However, if you are done exploring and ready to eat lunch or dinner, I recommend going to Yoder's Restaurant in the nearby Amish Village. Yoder's is well-known for its fried chicken and homemade pies. They don't serve the fried chicken on Fridays, so plan accordingly. Yoder's peanut butter pie (which has been in my refrigerator many times) was featured on the Travel Channel's "Man vs. Food."

It's a quick drive to Yoder's. Go back south onto U.S. 41. Make a left onto Bahia Vista Street. Yoder's will be less than two miles on your right-hand side of the road (watch your speed in this area).

Before leaving Selby Gardens, be sure to stop in the garden shop and bring home a bromeliad or an orchid.

Myakka River State Park, Sarasota

This "Live Like a Tourist" column has led to a shocking, disturbing discovery: I've been watching way too much bad television (if it has the word "real" or "swap," you can find it on my DVR) and way too little time exploring Florida.

I sometimes wonder what I've been doing for the last 13 years while people from across the pond (which is a terrible phrase because it's an enormously salty non-pond, but whatever) have already discovered places I'm only experiencing for the first time.

Exhibit A: Brian Barnett, from the London area, during a trip to Myakka River State Park.

"We've been to Florida six times. We always come here at least twice (during each trip)."

I've watched some episodes of "Real Housewives: New Jersey" at least twice... so I have that going for me.

Myakka River State Park serves as one of these eye-opening reminders to get off the couch and get outdoors.

It's an amazing park in Sarasot County. Myakka River State Park has the feel of a National Park due to its size, wildlife and amenities, but without the crowds that can interfere with your wildlife experience. After all, it's 58 square miles, so there's plenty of room to find your own space.

There are three must-do stops in the park (this does not include any of the hiking trails or the Myakka Outpost): the Birdwalk, the Canopy Walkway/Tower, and the bridge near the park entrance.

The Birdwalk is the farthest of the three from the entrance and reachable by driving. It's a long pier allowing guests access to

Live Like A Tourist ... in in the Great Outdoors

view the birds wading and feeding in the Upper Myakka Lake. This is a great place for birding and photography. Here, you can watch mighty osprey soar above the lake where alligators float by while herons search for lunch.

Another great spot for birding isn't on the map. It's the bridge near the Visitors Center and park entrance. It's a wide bridge, allowing enough room for vehicles to pass by while people standing along the edge take photos, use binoculars or watch the many varieties of birds socializing on a small island in the river. This also is one spot for a close encounter with alligators that like to bathe in the sun along the shore.

"It's great for the nature enthusiasts," said Todd Arcos, of Brevard, N.C. "I'm a bird-watching person, hardcore photographer."

The third amazing must-do at the park is the Canopy Walkway that leads to a tower that varies in height, depending on

If You Go

Where: Myakka River State Park, 13208 State Road 72, Sarasota
More info and additional costs: *www.floridastateparks. org/myakkariver/*
Tips: Wear sunscreen, mosquito repellent and comfortable shoes.

what you read. I'll go by the sign at the top of the tower stating 76.1 feet. The Canopy Walkway is one of only 17 in the U.S., according to an interesting sign at the base. Another sign warns guests that the walkway moves: "You can expect this walkway to sway as you cross it and the tall tower to shake when someone moves below. When the wind blows, the structure will rattle. Don't worry, it's only natural."

Both do shake, but the views are worth it. You are well above the treeline at the top of the tower where you can have an unobstructed, bird's eye view of the park.

Myakka River State Park is definitely a place requiring more than one visit. There are 39 miles of hiking trails and 20 miles of paved or dirt roads for biking. The park also can be viewed by water via kayak, canoe or airboat. Bicycles, kayaks and canoes can be rented.

There are a variety of camping options available such as historic cabins and sites for tents or RVs.

Those visiting for the day can grab lunch at the Myakka Outpost, which also sells a variety of souvenirs such as shirts, decorations and stuffed animals.

One thing is for sure: I need to know a little less about the "Real Housewives of New Jersey," and a little more about real residents of our state parks. Love it!

Myakka State Forest, Englewood

Some of you may have Fitbits. Or, perhaps, you purchased one or a similar fitness/activity tracker as part of a New Year's resolution/weight-loss plan.

I've been wearing one and it's depressing to see how much time I spend sitting… ugh.

For those who are unfamiliar, a Fitbit (which is what I have) tracks how many steps you take and miles you walk during a day. It knows your height, weight and gender, and it can then tell you how many calories you have burned each day. You also can track the food you have consumed, how you slept and any non-walking/running activities such as bicycling or swimming.

During an active day, my Fitbit will celebrate by vibrating on my wrist, alerting me to the fact that I have reached the calorie-burning goal.

I had several days in which I have walked more than 10,000 steps. But if you want to really challenge yourself, take a 7-year-old kid to Magic Kingdom. That day, we walked almost 25,000 steps for a total of 10.29 miles. "Zip-a-Dee-Doo-Dah" indeed! We went back to Magic Kingdom with a 2-year-old and 6-year-old in February, racking up another 7.11 miles in one day.

If you don't want to pay Disney prices or battle Disney crowds, head out to the Myakka State Forest to get your legs moving and your Fitbit going.

The 8,593-acre state forest, which kind of straddles the North Port-Englewood line at 2000 S. River Road, offers 13 miles of trails for hiking, bicycling or horseback riding.

For some reason, I wasn't paying attention to the lengths of the trails when I started off on my adventure.

I remember thinking, "this doesn't look too far," as I started walking down the wide, sunny North Loop Trail with one small bottle of water.

Live Like A Tourist … in in the Great Outdoors

The North Loop Trail actually covers more than 4 miles, and I was determined to see the campground site on the Myakka River, making for an extra long, but incredibly peaceful hike.

I was pleasantly surprised to find a campfire pit, picnic tables and even a small pier once I reached the river. Small campers and tents are allowed, but there is no electric or water available.

The Myakka State Forest is less expensive and less crowded than most state parks — especially the similarly named Myakka River State Park in Sarasota County. There, finding parking can be challenging and you'll likely see more people than wildlife (even though there are a lot of birds and alligators there).

What's worse than seeing a lot of people in nature? Hearing them.

One of my biggest pet peeves is hearing people loudly squawking, drowning out the sounds of chirping birds or splashing fish.

That's one of the reasons Myakka State Forest is special: It's so quiet that the sound of an armadillo rustling in palmettos seems amplified, and thus when rounding a corner I expected to see a Bengal tiger instead of the small rodent-like knight in armor.

Myakka State Forest is part of the state's Trailtrotter and Trailwalker programs. Those who choose to participate can earn credits toward merit patches. For more information on the Trailwalker program, go to *www.freshfromflorida.com/Divisions-Offices/Florida-Forest-Service/Recreation/Hiking*.

"The benefits are many when you participate in the Florida State Forests Trailwalker Program," states the website. "You get to improve your level of physical fitness at your own rate. Your only competitor is yourself. Also, you get to experience the beauty of Florida's State Forests. The opportunity to have personal experience with nature is rare these days, and this program will give you that opportunity."

Information about the Trailtrotter program also is available on the website — just click on "Horse Trails."

The Trailwalker program, or having my job or going to Disney World, is a great way to have fun while adding steps on your Fitbit.

By the day's end of my trip to the Myakka State Forest, I had logged 20,521 steps for a total of 8.43 miles… and no one asked me if I wanted to build a snowman or if I thought I could fly. And I kind of missed that. Oh well… until my next Disney visit, "Heigh-ho, heigh-ho. It's off to work I go."

Live Like A Tourist … **in the Great Outdoors**

Myakkahatchee Creek
Environmental Park, North Port

Real world worries of unpaid bills, unfinished chores and unreturned emails evaporate beneath a lush canopy of oak and palm trees.

Your blood pressure drops.

Your pulse slows.

Your shoulders relax.

Welcome to Myakkahatchee Creek Environmental Park.

One could go jogging, walking or bicycling past houses and cars in their neighborhood for exercise. Or, one could go jogging, walking or bicycling while exploring the 162-acre park in North Port.

Hmm… tough choice.

The Myakkahatchee Creek Environmental Park offers three trails: white, 0.73 miles; yellow, 1.58 miles; and red, 0.56 miles.

Live Like A Tourist ... **in in the Great Outdoors**

At the entrance on Reisterstown Road, there are picnic areas as well as a large trail map and informational sign offering images of the wildlife that may be seen in the park: red-shouldered hawks, sandhill cranes, Carolina willow, cabbage palm, saw palmetto, live oak, white-tailed deer, laurel oak, catbrier and alligators.

The longest trail, yellow, keeps visitors in the heart of the park. Walkers can hear some slight traffic noise at times, but the symphony of crickets, birds and flickering palms outweigh the man-made roar of a passing car.

I started out on the yellow trail, wandered onto the white trail, meandered back onto yellow, hiked onto the red trail, and found my way back to the yellow trail… I think. (Disclosure: I have absolutely no sense of direction. None.)

If you are like me — easily distracted and suffering from the sense of direction of a spastic bat awakened from a deep slumber — it's easy to lose yourself in the park. There are trail markers and signs guiding normal visitors along the way, but I do blame the park a little for my confusion because it's too beautiful.

Spanish moss adorns the oaks, acting like curtains dancing on an open window and providing a little extra protection from the sun. The footbridges lead visitors to photograph-worthy views of trees leaning into the creek — their branches trying to touch their own reflection in the water.

I didn't see any deer or alligators. I did, however, startle myself and a sounder of wild boar/hogs. Okay, I'll be honest: I looked like the bigger scaredy cat. They ran away while I started stomping and singing The Muppets' "Mahna Mahna." Clearly I have strange natural instincts in the wild.

It's a great park to take out-of-state guests so they can experience Old Florida. Plus, it's free.

If You Go

Where: Myakkahatchee Creek Environmental Park, 6968 Reisterstown Rd., North Port
Info: 941-861-5000

The park, which is managed by Sarasota County, also offers a canoe/kayak launch, but a lot of rainfall will be needed to make the creek navigable.

There is a primitive camping site as well, but reservations and permits are required.

For more information on camping or the park, call 941-861-5000.

Naples Botanical Garden, Naples

The year 2014 was a great one for the Naples Botanical Garden.

With the help of a $500,000 grant from the state's Division of Cultural Affairs along with donations, Naples Botanical Garden was able to build the impressive 25,000-square-foot Chabraja Visitor Center in addition to three gardens: LaGrippe Orchid, Kathryn's and Irma's. The $15 million project reopened in late October.

The 170-acre Garden, which is breathtakingly beautiful, "features the plants and cultures of the tropics and subtropics between the latitudes of 26 degrees North and 26 degrees South including Brazil, the Caribbean, Southeast Asia and Florida," states its website.

Sometimes a botanical garden can be boring for children, but the Naples attraction built an entire children's area, where kids can play in the water fountain/splash pad, Nancy and Jon Hamill's Cracker Cottage and Garden and treehouse. Children also are invited to leave behind their artwork in an area where chalk drawings are encouraged in the Vicky C. and David Byron Smith Children's Garden.

The Pfeffer-Beach Butterfly Garden is located nearby, where Florida species of butterflies can be viewed and photographed.

The estate offers a variety of gardens that concentrate on regions such as Florida, Brazil, Caribbean and Asia.

The Kapnick Caribbean Garden is one of my favorites. There, you'll find a lawn for bocce ball playing, a Coral Stone Pergola decorated with Queens Wreath vine, which is a replica of a pergola at "Andromeda Garden in Barbados, former home of Iris Bannochie, one of the Caribbean's most influential horticulturists," states the website. The Caribbean Garden, created by American landscape architect Robert Truskowski, also offers a relaxing beach area where guests can take a nap in a hammock.

Kathleen and Scott Kapnick Brazilian Garden offers one of the most beautiful views of the garden, where one can see flowers and trees reflecting in the pond while feeling relaxed by the sound of the waterfall.

One of my other favorite areas is the Florida Garden, and the nearby Succulent Garden, Wildflower Meadow, Idea Garden and Enabling Garden. These areas, in particular, offer a lot of ideas as to what you may want to do at your home.

While the trees, plants, air plants and flowers are the main attractions, I was pleasantly surprised to see so much wildlife. Who knew it would be a great place for birding? The Naples Botanical Garden folks, apparently, because they added a birding tower that looks over a lake toward the Florida Garden. Keep an eye out for alligators and rabbits in addition to a variety of birds.

Entry into the garden includes a map, which lists walking trails and the distances so that, for example, walkers know they will be covering a little over a mile if they walk the entire Lake Trail. There also is a cafe and gift shop.

If you plan to go to the Naples Botanical Garden, consider doing so while the Night Lights are going on during the holidays.

Expect to hear music, enjoy a glass of wine, and wander the garden after dark, where palm trees are illuminated with Christmas lights and even lasers. Other trees are lighted in such a way that allows visitors to see details they wouldn't ordinarily see in natural light.

Naples Botanical Garden is beautiful during the day and during Night Lights — so be sure to add this to your list of places to visit soon in Southwest Florida.

Oscar Scherer State Park, Osprey

When relatives visit, kids are home from school, and dogs are chasing their tails, the once 2,000 square feet of home now seems to be 500 square feet of "Alice in Wonderland" claustrophobia.

It's time to step outside and breathe.

Oscar Scherer State Park, off U.S. 41 in Osprey, is a beautiful, inexpensive place to escape the family or to bring the family.

The 1,300-plus acres offer hiking trails of varied lengths, campgrounds, kayak/canoe rentals, wildlife watching, informational Nature Center and a lake for swimming (for those brave enough to risk being alligator bait).

There are two main areas of the park and both should be explored. I recommend driving to the farthest parking area first, which is near Lake Osprey and Nature Center.

The Nature Center, or visitor center as it's also called, offers an orientation of the park. There are three short videos that provide information about the park and its inhabitants. There's a very interesting diorama of a gopher tortoise's habitat, and the other critters that may be found in the hole as well. The Nature Center also sells souvenirs. In case you forgot to bring water, drinks are available from the vending machine.

As you walk outside the Nature Center, take a quick hike on the trail that loops Osprey Lake. Keep an eye out for alligators, but more importantly, keep an ear out for birds that may be squawking or singing above your head. If it's warm and you're so inclined, take a dip in the lake (I did not as I maintain a healthy respect/fear of alligators).

Once you are done exploring this end of the park, drive back to the South Creek Picnic Area. This is where you can put in canoes/kayaks as well as stroll through

the Lester Finley Trail. This is the easiest of the trails to navigate. It winds along the water, offering chances to hear fish jumping, birds talking and squirrels scrambling up trees.

Bring a lunch as there are numerous picnic tables around the park. There also are playgrounds near both of the parking areas.

Live Like A Tourist ... in in the Great Outdoors

There are a variety of trails offered at Oscar Scherer State Park. Here is some information on the six trails, as provided in the trail brochure handed to you at the Ranger Station:

If You Go

Where: Oscar Scherer State Park, 1843 S. Tamiami Trail, Osprey

More info: *www. floridastateparks.org/ oscarscherer*

Tips: Wear comfortable shoes and bring water

- Yellow (5 miles for bicyclists and hikers): "It is 5 miles of mainly level and sandy trails. … It passes through mesic pine flatwoods, prairie hammocks, and scrubby flatwoods."
- Blue Trail (1.5 miles for bicyclists and hikers): "It passes through the mesic pine flatwoods and scrubby flatwoods. It begins at the same trailhead as the Red Trail and then follows the fence line north along a housing development… Much of the trail can be sandy in dry weather and provides little shade during the hike."
- Red Trail (2 miles for bicyclists and hikers): "Explores the northwestern portion of the park… It begins at the same trailhead as the Blue Trail and later splits off following the boundary of the park along a housing development to the western boundary."
- Green Trail (3 miles for bicyclists and hikers): "It can be either a 2- or a 3-mile hike by following the marked trails but several well-marked service roads allow many self-determined routes through scrubby flatwoods and mesic pine flatwoods… It is the best biking trail in the park." I hiked a portion of this, and I can see how it would be fun for biking.
- Lester Finley Trail (half-mile for hikers only): "The Lester Finley Trail meanders through a hardwood hammock along a tidal reach of South Creek, a blackwater stream that eventually empties into Dryman Bay. This is a 'barrier-free' trail offering superb hiking opportunities for those with disabilities. … There is a handicapped equipped fishing pier, two butterfly gardens, several benches, two picnic tables, and a water fountain along the trail. Additionally, there are five audio boxes along the trail that explain various aspects of the different habitats." This is a must-do for all visitors.
- South Creek Nature Trail (half-mile for hikers only): "Several markers along the trail point out aspects of the natural environment. An extensive tree canopy provides shade during the midday heat."

Paynes Creek Historic State Park, Bowling Green

Florida State Parks are as varied as the critters that inhabit them.

Myakka River State Park encompasses thousands of acres of wildlife. Stump Pass Beach State Park boasts beautiful, postcard views of the Gulf of Mexico.

Then there's Paynes Creek Historic State Park in Bowling Green. It's a smaller park, occupying about 410 acres. While many of Florida's 171 state parks have interesting histories, Paynes Creek is one of only 31 that are designated as historic sites, according to the state park's website.

Paynes Creek's roots date back to the 1840s, when an interior trading post was needed.

"Built in early 1849, the post was attacked and destroyed by renegade Indians that summer," states the website. "In late 1849, Fort Chokonikla was built nearby as the first outpost in a chain of forts established to control the Seminoles. The Seminoles never attacked the fort, but the Army was nearly defeated by mosquitoes."

The first stop should be to the Visitors Center, where guests can learn about this history.

"The historic events at this site occurred in 1849-1850, between the Second and Third Seminole Wars," states a sign in the Visitors Center.

Live Like A Tourist ... in in the Great Outdoors

Not much remains of these early days, but there is a monument honoring Capt. George S. Payne and Dempsey Whiddon, who were killed by the Seminoles on July 17, 1849.

The park's well-maintained, well-marked trails cross white sand, grass, pavement and even a suspension bridge and a wooden catwalk.

The Fort Chokonikla Trail is an easy, quarter-mile trail near the Visitors Center, where guests can see empty lands that once housed three blockhouses and canvas tents.

The Peace River Trail is a longer trail, which takes visitors along the quiet Paynes Creek and to the Peace River. There is a canoe/kayak launch in the park, but see the ranger for access.

A visit to this park, which is listed on the National Registry of Historic Places, can be a half-day or full-day adventure as there are picnicking areas, a playground and other trails as well.

Ponce de Leon Park, Punta Gorda

There's Chickie-pants, the sandhill crane with a crisscrossed beak.

There's Luna, the abandoned white screech owl who is leucistic.

Then there's the 10 acres of beautiful waterfront park property that offers something for everyone... and homes to Chickie-pants, Luna and about 100 of their buddies at the Peace River Wildlife Center at Ponce de Leon Park.

The Wildlife Center and park are two-for-one gems in Punta Gorda.

Ponce de Leon may be one of the most beautiful parks in the area. It provides many amenities despite its small size. Boaters quickly can access the creek, harbor and gulf from the boat ramp. There's a small beach area for those looking to tan or watch the sunset. There are areas to fish and kayak. There is a small, quarter-mile boardwalk, which takes visitors through the mangroves and provides information about wildlife. There also is a playground for kids, and even an outdoor chapel for weddings.

Across the parking lot is the other must-see attraction, the Peace River Wildlife Center.

Tours are offered daily, and be sure to say hi to Chickie-pants.

"He came to us as a fledgling," said Callie Stahl, operations manager for the wildlife center.

While helping a sandhill crane that got stuck in a fence about a year ago, rescuers saw Chickie-pants with its crisscrossed beak. It's a common occurrence that worsens with age, Callie said.

Live Like A Tourist ... in in the Great Outdoors

The crisscrossed beak makes him difficult for it to seek out insects to eat.

"He eats from a bucket," Callie said. "He wouldn't have that ability in the wild."

Although it can be sad to look at Chickie-pants' crisscrossed beak, it's very educational and inspiring to see these animals being cared for by loving employees and volunteers. It's more sad to wonder where these creatures would be without the center.

Luna, for one, likely wouldn't be alive.

The white screech owl is leucistic, which means it is white as snow. And since we have no snow, Luna has no ability to blend into his surroundings.

"We think his family kicked him out of the nest because he didn't look like them," Callie said. "He has absolutely no camouflage."

Luna has become the educational ambassador for the Wildlife Center, which takes in about 1,900 to 2,000 animals each year.

If You Go

Where: Peace River Wildlife Center and Ponce de Leon Park, 3400 Ponce de Leon Parkway, Punta Gorda

More info: Park, 941-575-5050; Center, 941-637-3830 or *www.peaceriverwildlifecenter.com*

The wildlife center sees a lot of baby birds in the spring.

"In May, we got in 165 birds," Callie said. "The majority were babies."

Some are brought in after nests are disturbed. Some were dropped by predators knocking down nests. Some are blown out of nests during storms. And some, like Luna, are deserted by their families.

About 40 percent of the animals brought into the wildlife center will be rehabbed and released.

Others become permanent residents, like Chickie-pants and Luna, along with eagles, pelicans, owls, hawks, tortoises, etc.

The wildlife center also has a great gift shop with T-shirts, stuffed animals, jewelry, books and other items that make for great presents while supporting a good cause.

Those wanting to help the center can adopt an animal or become a member.

The wildlife center also has a wish list of items that includes aluminum cans, balls (tennis, racquet or whiffle), raw eggs, finch seed (with millet, not just thistle; no sunflower seeds), carrots, fruit (grapes, apples, melons), greens (romaine, spring mix, kale), hanging parrot toys, baby toys, paper towels, UVA/UVB light bulbs and jars of baby food. For the complete list, go to *www.peaceriverwildlifecenter.com/wishlist.html.*

Sarasota Jungle Gardens, Sarasota

There are one-of-a-kind places that likely could only exist in Florida: The Shell Factory, Gatorland, Linger Lodge.

The Sarasota Jungle Gardens should be on that list.

This is another great place to take kids while they are on winter break — especially elementary school-aged kids.

The Sarasota Jungle Gardens opened on New Year's Eve in 1939. Initially, it was just a botanical garden, which still exists today.

"Some of our prized possessions include the rare Australian nut tree, a bunya bunya tree, the largest Norfolk Island pine in Florida, bulrush, strangler figs, royal palms, selloums, banana trees, Peruvian apple cactus, staghorn ferns and native red maples, oak trees and bald cypress," according to the gardens' website.

Take time to explore the gardens. A map will be provided upon entry. There are easy-to-navigate paths that weave around animal exhibits, playgrounds, waterfalls and other attractions. There are plenty of benches scattered around, as well, for those who want to take a break, rest their feet, or simply enjoy the view.

The famous bird shows were added in the 1970s, and they remain a highlight today. Don't miss the Jungle Bird Show. Show times, of course, are subject to change, so check for any updated times when

Live Like A Tourist ... in in the Great Outdoors

Where: Sarasota Jungle Gardens. 3701 Bay Shore Road, Sarasota

More info: *www. sarasotajunglegardens.com* or 941-355-5305

you arrive. The Jungle Bird Show is the one in which you can see birds roller-skate, making you feel a little clumsy if you are unable to do so. Little kids, especially in the preschool/kindergarten ages, seemed to be mesmerized by the brightly colored macaws as they interact with the audience.

There are other non-bird shows throughout the day as well.

The Gardens also offer a Wild Life Wonder Show: "Learn about red-tailed hawks, kookaburras, owls, skunks, hissing cockroaches and so many more. The dynamics of this show change frequently, and you never know which animal will make an appearance. We promise you'll be thoroughly entertained by all things creeping, crawling and wiggling," the website states.

For a tamer form of entertainment, be sure to spend some time with the pink flamingos, located near the center of the gardens. Food can be purchased to hand-feed the funny birds. The people-friendly birds are celebrities (sort of). There's a live flamingo camera recording their movements that can be viewed online at *www.sarasotajunglegardens.com.*

In addition to the flamingos, macaws and reptiles, expect to see a crocodile, prairie dogs, lemurs, monkeys and butterflies, as well as other critters.

Those needing a midday snack or lunch can purchase food in the Flamingo Cafe.

Before leaving, stop in the gift shop. It may be a good place to find a last-minute Christmas present or a souvenir to remember your fun day at the Sarasota Jungle Gardens.

Six Mile Cypress Slough Preserve, Fort Myers

Ssshhhhhh.

How else can you hear a boat-tailed grackle squawk?

How else can you hear the splash of an anhinga diving?

How else can you hear the snort of an alligator or hog?

To put it kindly: You are missing out on the amazing sounds and sights of nature if you're jabbering on a nature trail.

To put it bluntly: Zip it. You are ruining our nature experience.

Lee County Parks & Recreation does a great job educating people about human noise. First of all, it posts this message on its website: "Please respect the space and quiet observation needs of individual

visitors by LIMITING CELLPHONE USE on trail to emergencies only." The message is reiterated on the trails as well.

Lee County more subtly suggests silence on its "tips for finding wildlife page":

1. "Be as quiet as possible" ... OK, not too subtle.

2. "Walk slowly... Slowing your pace automatically quiets your walk." Hmmm... a common theme is emerging.

3. "Watch for movement and listen" ... And there you have it.

Having been to several parks now in Charlotte, Sarasota, DeSoto and Lee counties, I've come across human squawkers on nature trails. Having seen Lee County's not-so-subtle reminders, I felt the need to share its educational message.

Most visitors to Six Mile Cypress Slough Preserve in Fort Myers behaved

respectfully on the 1.2-mile boardwalk nature trail. After hearing a female parrot with a New York accent on the trail, I simply waited about five minutes and continued on my way — distancing myself from Polly wanting a cracker.

Live Like A Tourist ... **in in the Great Outdoors**

Six Mile Cypress Slough Preserve offers one of the best nature trails in Southwest Florida.

It is slightly raised, allowing for a safer feeling (even though we all know snakes can still slither their scary bodies up onto the boardwalk). It's also an even surface, making it easier for those who have trouble walking. There are benches along the way, too, so visitors can rest their feet or enjoy nature from a quiet, seated position.

Before you even get to the trail, however, you will notice a cleverly designed parking lot.

If You Go

Where: Six Mile Cypress Slough Preserve, 7751 Penzance Blvd., Fort Myers

Tips: Bring water and mosquito repellent

More info: 239-533-7550 or *https://www.leegov.com/parks/facility?fid=0105*

A pavilion isn't just a covered picnic area here. At Six Mile Cypress, the pavilion's roof is a great blue heron's wing. A bike rack isn't a boring, silver rectangle with bars. Here, it's a bright-colored alligator.

The park also offers a free, fascinating Interpretive Center, which isn't a typical two-dimensional center with photos of wildlife that can be seen in the preserve. Instead, it allows you to hear the sounds some animals make. It provides a display of hides so you can feel the softness of a bobcat. It offers a Halloween-like exhibit, in which you can put your hand in a box to blindly feel an object (I was too chicken, but I noticed one of the items was a portion of a deer's antler).

The volunteers on hand are knowledgeable and friendly, as are the ones along the trail.

Take your time on the trail and use the Explorer's Companion (offered on-site or online: *http://www.leegov.com/parks/Documents/Explorers-Companion.pdf*). There are informational signs, as well as inspirational quotes along the way. Painters, writers and nature lovers will love exploring the boardwalk, which winds its way through the preserve to Pop Ash Pond, Gator Lake, Otter Pond and Wood Duck Pond.

If you go, expect to hear and see active birds. During one afternoon, I saw at least one of the following creatures: a red-tailed hawk, boat-tailed grackle, anhinga, alligator, turtle, squirrel and cottonmouth (ooh, scary). There were many other kinds of birds as well.

Enjoy Six Mile Cypress Slough Preserve, its wildlife, its boardwalk, its Interpretive Center and even its parking lot.

And remember Lee County's tip: "Be as quiet as possible." After all, no one wants to go hiking with the Real Housewives of New York, New Jersey, Orange County, etc.

Live Like A Tourist ... in the Great Outdoors

Stump Pass Beach State Park, Englewood

Georgina McCurley looked down as she walked along the water's edge at Stump Pass Beach State Park.

The black specks in the sand captured McCurley's attention on a spring morning. Unbeknownst to her, a manatee swam by along with several schools of cownose rays.

It's easy to miss a gift from nature on this Englewood beach. There are simply too many treasures to see: shells, shark teeth, stingrays, manatees, jumping fish, pelicans, shore birds, rolling waves, etc.

McCurley, of Canada, regularly visits Englewood's four beaches (Stump Pass Beach, Englewood Beach, Blind Pass, known as Middle Beach, and Manasota Beach).

"This one is the most beautiful beach because of the trees at the end," she said.

I'm embarrassed to admit I had never been to Stump Pass Beach. I've lived in Charlotte County for more than 10 years.

Seems like a crime, I know. There's this unbelievable mile of gorgeous, pristine beach in my own county and I neglected it for more than a decade.

Shame on me.

Now that I've been there, I want to go back already.

Robert and Theresa Woolsey live life the right way. The Canadians spend

Live Like A Tourist ... in in the Great Outdoors

six months a year in Englewood, and they spend nearly every day of that time visiting Stump Pass Beach.

"We just love it," Robert said.

The Woolseys go to many islands along the coast from Sarasota to Fort Myers via their pontoon boat.

"We love Englewood the best," Robert said. "It's just beautiful."

What's great about Stump Pass Beach, as opposed to other Gulf beaches, is that you can disappear along an undeveloped beach. No houses. No bars. No condos.

If You Go

Where: Stump Pass Beach State Park, 900 Gulf Blvd., Englewood
Tips: There is not much parking, so either get there early or plan to wait/stalk.
For more information: *www. floridastateparks.org/stumppass/* or 941-964-0375

When you pull into the parking lot, it may seem like a crowded beach because parking fills up quickly. However, the farther south you walk along the beach, the fewer people you see.

Suddenly, you can find yourself alone (except for the passing shell collector or fisherman) on your own private patch of beach.

Stump Pass Beach seems perfect for snorkeling, fishing and kayaking. (I only dipped in my feet, but the warm water was crystal clear. I plan to return on a day off from work to explore the water more.)

There are picnic tables as well as walking trails with informational signs. (Note to those picnicking: Be sure to get food on Manasota Key or before getting to the island.)

And, of course, the beach is great for shelling.

"I love the shells," said Linda Marshall of Gloucester, Mass., as she dipped her hand in the shell-laden sand. "The shells bring me here and the sharks teeth."

Christine McGuire of Danvers, Mass., said the lure of Stump Pass Beach State Park is the Caribbean-colored water. She looked out over the patches of emerald-green and dark-blue waters, spotting a school of cownose rays in the surf.

Whether it's the colorful water, the wildlife, the shelling or the fishing or good, old-fashioned peace, Stump Pass State Beach Park truly is one of the most beautiful beaches in all of Southwest Florida.

Sunken Gardens, St. Petersburg

Across from modern-day Panera Bread, with its flatbreads and paninis, is an old-style, Florida-kitschy, gaudy-in-a-good-way sign that reads: "Beautiful Sunken Gardens."

Sunken Gardens provides a few city blocks of tranquility in the middle of a bustling St. Petersburg neighborhood.

"It's hard to imagine that all this can be going on right off Fourth Street," wrote a 2015 reviewer on TripAdvisor, which lists Sunken Gardens among the top attractions. "It has so much to offer and is much larger than one would think."

That's the beauty of Sunken Gardens: Like so much in life and in nature, there's so much more than meets the eye.

A plumber named George Turner Sr. bought the property in 1903.

"He drained a shallow lake that dropped 15 feet below street level to provide a rich soil to grow fruits and exotic plants from all over the world," states the flier. "By 1924, his amazing garden was attracting visitors who paid 25 cents for a stroll through the beautiful, lush gardens."

"Three generations of the Turner family continued the vision that created this unique tropical garden, with its flowing ponds," states the website.

The city of St. Petersburg bought Sunken Gardens in 1999.

Live Like A Tourist ... in in the Great Outdoors

"Preserving the garden was a community effort," states the city's website. "With Mr. Turner Sr.'s original vision in mind, the city's goal is to preserve this historic botanical garden and provide cultural and educational opportunities."

Today, there are more than 50,000 tropical flowers and plants scattered around the park, which is easy to navigate along paved pathways. There also are nearly 100 varieties of crotons, which are "genetically unstable tropical plants that originated in the Molluca Islands of Indonesia," explained signage in the Gardens. There also are areas designated for beautiful, blooming orchids; blossoming water lilies in a pond; and cascading waterfalls providing a soundtrack accented by the occasional squawk or chirp.

When strolling the grounds, do so slowly or you'll miss the smallest, most active creatures of the Gardens. Bees constantly buzz around from flower to flower. The shadows of rapid butterflies fluttering above will catch your eye as well. And if you close your eyes, you'll likely hear the rustling sounds of squirrels high up in a tree.

If You Go

Where: Sunken Gardens, 1825 4th St. N., St. Petersburg
More info: *www.stpete.org/ attractions/sunken_gardens/ index.php* or 727-551-3102

Of course, there are the more docile residents: the colorful redfooted tortoise and the dinosaur-looking alligator snapping turtle, which (trivia fact of the day) is a threatened species and the largest freshwater turtle in North America, according to National Geographic.

There also are caged birds as well as the free-roaming ones, which smartly chose a small piece of paradise in a big city.

The Turner family's legacy extends beyond the petals and branches as well.

"The main building on Fourth Street was built in 1926 and became the Coca-Cola Bottling Company in the 1940s," states the website. "The Turner family purchased the building in 1967 to create the World's Largest Gift Shop and the King of Kings Wax Museum. They closed the building in 1995. The city has restored it to its original Mediterranean Revival style and it is the new home for Great Explorations, a children's science museum."

Entry into Great Explorations is an additional fee, but it's a good way to cool off with children after exploring Sunken Gardens.

Live Like A Tourist ... in the Great Outdoors

. . . During Happy Hour

Celtic Ray,
Punta Gorda

There are some places that have the feel of an old friend's house, where good times with those who know you (and still love you) lead to rich Kodachrome memories.

That's the Celtic Ray, where a whiff of vinegar can lead to a far-off gaze down the memory highway where a perfectly poured Black and Tan serves as the landmark to a once-forgotten evening of coleslaw silliness.

That's the Celtic Ray, where the faint sound of a fiddle triggers instant relaxation lingering from one afternoon in the sun, sipping a pint as Brigid's Cross plays "I'm Your Mailman," "Twelve" or even "Sweet Caroline."

Ba ba baaa.

That's the Celtic Ray.

The Punta Gorda pub, 145 E. Marion Ave., is more than a restaurant or a bar. It can be an experience. You can go for live music, comedy night, trivia or open mic night. Or you can go when there is no entertainment, enjoy conversations with friends or strangers, or bring a book/e-reader/tablet/laptop and unwind.

Live Like A Tourist ... **During Happy Hour**

For first-timers, let me give you a few tips:

1. Order your drinks and food at the bar (like at a pub in Ireland).
2. The menu is written on the boards near the bar.
3. Yes, the beer may seem pricey, but remember, you are getting a pint of really good beer (not a plastic cup of Natty Light).
4. Don't try ordering Natty Light.
5. Yes, it may seem a little dark inside. But your eyes will adjust. And remember, we're all better looking in the dark.

The Celtic Ray has been serving its famous fish and chips since 1997. The fish (crisp, yet moist) and chips (also known as fries) are amazing. Please try it with the pub vinegar before dipping in tartar sauce and ketchup (though I've been known to do that too). If you aren't a fan of fish, there are plenty of other good choices as well.

Kevin Doyle and his son, Max, have made the Celtic Ray one of the best pubs in Southwest Florida (if not the entire state).

Stop in and enjoy the experience.

If you don't trust me, check out the high praise the Celtic Ray receives on Google Reviews, Yelp, Trip Advisor and Urbanspoon.

If You Go

Where: Celtic Ray, 145 E. Marion Ave., Punta Gorda
More info: 941-916-9115, *http://celticray.net* or check them out on Facebook.

Fat Point,
Punta Gorda

Beer used to be just that: beer.

While I worked on a bachelor's degree in English, I minored in general beer consumption. The name didn't matter, nor did the taste. It could have been Miller Lite, Budweiser, Keystone Light, Natural Light, Red Dog — it simply didn't matter as long as the beer was cheap, or even better, free.

I've graduated from the days of drinking fraternity beer, though I'm still far from being a sophisticated beer connoisseur.

The beer industry has evolved as well in the last few decades, and craft brewers are becoming big players.

Example: Fat Point Brewing in Punta Gorda.

Co-owners Bill Frazer and Duncan Scarry started brewing the first beers in Punta Gorda in August 2014. They opened the Fat Point taproom in February in 2015.

"We are already operating at capacity," said Bill, who graduated from Lemon Bay High School in 1998. "It's incredible. We've doubled our forecast."

Bill didn't start his career in the beer industry. He attended the General Motors Institute in Michigan, which is now known as Kettering University. He worked in

Live Like A Tourist ... **During Happy Hour**

Where: Fat Point, 611 Charlotte
St., Punta Gorda
More info: 800-380-7405,
sales@fatpoint.com or
www.fatpoint.com

the engineering field in Washington, D.C., and then in Los Angeles.

"That's when I started to get into different beer, craft beer," Bill said.

California, however, was saturated with craft brewers. In fact, California ranks first in the country for the highest number of craft brewers. According to the Brewers Association's State Craft Beer Sales & Production Statistics for 2013, California housed 381 craft brewers, which produced more than 2.9 million barrels of craft beer. By comparison, Florida had only 66 craft brewers, according to the same report.

"There was such a void out here," Bill said.

His family still lived in the area, and the decision was made to open Charlotte County's craft brewery.

He brought with him four of the popular beers he created in California: Ryeght Angle IPA, Big Boca Ale, Bru Man Chu and Chorange Stout.

Now, there are other beers such as Putsin Pale Ale, Kickback Kolsch and my fave J-Dawg Porter.

"It was either going to take off, or it was going to burn," he said.

Oh, it took off, all right. There already are plans to expand.

Fat Point Brewing isn't just a bar. It's a destination. It's a place to take friends and out-of-towners, who can't experience a Bru Man Chu in Michigan.

There are a few table games inside the clean, sleek-looking silver taproom such as Connect Four and Cards Against Humanity. There also are large televisions surrounding the bar for sports fans. Outside, where leashed dogs are allowed, there's a giant Jenga, bocce ball and cornhole.

There are normally eight to 10 beers on tap. First-timers should consider ordering a flight, which allows you to pick four 4-ounce beers. This is a great way to find your favorite. Fat Point also offers a few food items such as excellent pretzels, pizzas, pigs in a blanket and some special sandwiches.

Fat Point actively posts updates on its Facebook page. It also has a newsletter that beer fans can sign up for on its website, *www.fatpoint.com.*

Hofbräuhaus, St. Petersburg

"Zicke zacke, zicke zacke, hoi hoi hoi!" Oktoberfest provides a perfectly acceptable excuse for chanting that fun cheer before consuming German beers and devouring wursts.

Danke, Germans, for your beers, wursts, pretzels and hilarious translation of the word butterfly, Schmetterling.

Now, there's even more good news for beer-drinking, pretzel-loving fools like me. The famous Hofbräuhaus, originally located in Munich, Germany, has opened a St. Petersburg restaurant/ beer hall/beer garden.

Hofbräuhaus' roots date back to 1589.

"Wilhelm V, the Duke of Bavaria (1579-1597), had a thirsty and demanding household," states the website. "They were dissatisfied with the beer brewed in Munich, and so beer had to be imported from the town of Einbeck in Lower Saxony."

His peeps, as I'm sure he'd call them now, suggested building their own brewery.

"Wilhelm was delighted with the idea and on the very same day... recruited the brewmaster of Geisenfeld Monastery, Heimeran Pongraz, to plan and supervise the construction of Hofbräuhaus (the 'ducal brewery'), and to be its first master brewer."

Thus, Hofbräuhaus in Munich was born... making generations of livers and stomachs very happy.

I'm fortunate to have enjoyed a beer and pretzel in the original Munich Hofbräuhaus, which is a massive hall packed with tourists and locals.

Hofbräuhaus isn't the kind of place where you order a Bud or a Miller... please don't be *that* American in Hofbräuhaus.

The three year-round beers are as follows:

- Original: My favorite. It's an extremely smooth lager that goes down like water... better than water. The alcohol content is about 5.1 percent.

Live Like A Tourist ... **During Happy Hour**

- Dunkel: A dark brown beer that actually was the first beer in the brewery's history. The alcohol content is about 5.5 percent.
- Hefe Weizen: A wheat beer that is about 5.1 percent alcohol.

The three seasonal beers are:
- Oktoberfest: "Offering 6.3 percent alcohol by volume and a clean, crisp edge, it is a vital part of the Oktoberfest experience. As unique as the Oktoberfest itself," states the website.
- Hefe Weizen Dunkel: "Combining refreshing notes of wheat beer and the richness of dark beer, Hefe Weizen Dunkel creates a wonderful and unique flavor," states the website. "This one-of-a-kind beer is fermented similarly to light beer and stored in kegs for about one week, but in a way as unique as its flavor: upside down! Just before tapping time the yeast redistributes by turning the keg upright."
- Maibock: "By tradition, the first barrel of Maibock is tapped at the Hofbräuhaus in the last week of April, in time for the merry month of May. The success story of Munich's oldest bock beer goes back as far as 1614," states the website. Be careful drinking this one as the alcohol content is about 7.2 percent.

As for the food, I recommend the Sausage Tower, which is a three-tier creation straight from heaven. The tower offers a variety of sausages and the bottom plate is fresh pretzels. Mmm…

The new St. Petersburg Hofbräuhaus is the closest one to Southwest Florida. Other locations in the United States include:
- Newport, Ky.: Check, check, check (I've been there a few times).
- Las Vegas: Check, check (I've been there twice).
- Pittsburgh
- Chicago
- Cleveland
- Columbus
- Panama City Beach
- St. Petersburg: Check (I've been there once now, but I'll be back).

As you venture to Oktoberfest events or to Hofbräuhaus, you'll want to know this toast:

"Ein Prosit, ein Prosit
"Der Gemütlichkeit
"Ein Prosit, ein Prosit
"Der Gemütlichkeit."

If You Go

Where: Hofbräuhaus St. Petersburg, 123 Fourth St. South
More info: *www. hofbrauhausstpetersburg.com* or 727-898-3333

Live Like A Tourist … **During Happy Hour**

Linger Lodge, Bradenton

There's an old Florida restaurant on the Braden River that uses snakes to form the letters of the restaurant's name. This same place has "Chunk of Skunk" on its menu, just above "Swirl of Squirrel" and "Poodles 'n' Noodles." There's also a human leg hanging out of an alligator's mouth.

"Take a gander," said David LaRusso, general manager of Linger Lodge. "This is a part of Florida you don't normally see."

That's true. ... This is the only place I've seen where snakes spell out "Linger Lodge." And that's probably a good thing. After all, can you imagine how many snakes it would take to spell out Michelangelo Pizzeria & Italian Restaurant or Mary Margaret's Tea & Biscuit? (And I don't even want to think about how long the snake would need to be to form the ampersand.)

Forbes named Linger Lodge one of the "Top 10 Most Unusual Restaurants in the World."

Al Roker called it one of the "Top Five Weirdest Restaurants in America."

How about that? One of the weirdest, most unusual restaurants in the world is right here in Southwest Florida.

Linger Lodge, which also has a campground, cabins, boat/kayak launch, is a great place to take out-of-state loved ones for some Snake Bites, Swamp Water or Braden River Tea (fruity adult drinks — I recommend the Linger Lizard).

The restaurant's bizarreness slithers right out of the menu — especially in the portion that is meant as a joke. There, customers

Live Like A Tourist ... **During Happy Hour**

are offered the "Bag 'N' Gag: Our daily takeout lunch special. ... Anything dead on bread. ... Eating food is more fun when you know it was hit on the run."

This part of the menu also offers Tummy Teasers that include Chunk of Skunk, Road toad a la mode and Rigor Mortis Tortoise among others. The last joke section offers Canine Cuisine (my dogs Lucky and Cosmo Kramer should stop reading now): Slab of Lab, Cocker Cutlets and German Shepherd Pie.

The real menu is just as quirky, and presumably far more tasty than Pit Bull Pot Pie.

The specialty is Linger Lodge Etouffee, which is described as: "Traditional New Orleans style Etouffee with a Linger flair — Andouille sausage, chicken, crawfish, shrimp and mussels in our 'Award winning' gumbo served over white rice with garlic bread."

I'm a huge fan of New Orleans and go there about once a year, so I chose not to try the Etouffee and instead opted for more Florida-ish food... like alligator.

If You Go

Where: Linger Lodge, 7205 85th St. Court E., Bradenton
More info: 941-755-2757 or *www.lingerlodgeresort.com*
Tips: Eat outside — there are fans so it's not too hot. There is a gluten-free menu. Also, if you go during season, make a reservation.

Linger Lodge offers gator meat in a variety of ways. I went with the Alligator Chowder, which was really tasty and actually bites back at you. I also ordered the Snake Back Onion Rings with Venom Sauce. There's something for everyone: salads, burgers, fish, etc.

No matter what you eat, I'm warning you now: Save room for dessert (and I'm not a big dessert eater).

I tried the River Bed Pie: "A bed of crumbled Oreo's, vanilla ice cream, chocolate fudge, whipped cream, cherries and walnuts." It was like a bowl full of heaven delivered to my table. I think I even heard angels singing, although it was more likely alligators crooning — seriously, it's that good. It's also enormous, so share it.

For a place that prides itself on Old Florida-style, you wouldn't expect modern menu items, but Linger Lodge offers a large gluten-free menu for those with dietary restrictions.

There is a boat ramp and kayak launch right outside the restaurant so it's reachable by land and by sea... err, by river.

Rosa Fiorelli Winery & Vineyard, Bradenton

When it comes to wine, many people think of Italy, France or California.

Indeed, California produces the most wine in the United States. In fact, it churned out more than 728 million gallons in 2013, according to the Department of the Treasury's Alcohol and Tobacco Tax and Trade Bureau.

Surprisingly, Florida is one of the country's top wine producers as well.

So where are Florida's wineries?

One of the closest is the Rosa Fiorelli Winery & Vineyard in Bradenton, which (depending upon the weather) produces about 1,500 to 2,000 gallons a year, said Sal Fiorelli.

Sal's parents, Antonio and Rosa, moved from Casteldaccia, Sicily, to Manatee County, and started the winery in 1998. They began with just a few vines of grapes, and have since expanded to 10 acres and built a 3,000-square-foot winery, which can be toured.

"He had a love for wine and for making wine," Sal said during a tour.

Sal wasn't always in the wine business. He had been working in claims adjusting when his dad died in 2013. Sal left his job and joined the family's winery and vineyard. He now sounds like a chemistry professor who moonlights as a sommelier, (which is a trained wine expert for the beer drinkers out there like me).

The muscadine grapes, which are native to Florida, are hand-picked each summer during the earliest, coolest time of the day. Some are harvested as early as June while other varieties are picked closer to September.

"We pick our fruit when it is fresh and vibrant and sweet and fruitiest," Sal said.

Live Like A Tourist ... **During Happy Hour**

They don't stomp on the grapes with their feet like Lucille Ball — although they do offer that activity during some special events like the annual Harvest Festival. No, you won't be drinking that foot-stomped wine.

During the tour, Sal goes into great detail about the fermentation, which made me regret my lack of effort in chemistry class in high school. Once the wine is ready to be bottled, the fun begins again in the winery with many people helping during that process. The winery can fill eight bottles in one minute, and each receives a specialized cork "to provide a very nice seal," Sal said. The staff also labels its own bottles.

Wine-making is a year-round production. Vines need to be pruned. New vines need to be propagated. Critters aren't too much of a problem for the Bradenton vineyard, but hail last year damaged a few hundred pounds of grapes, Sal said.

The following states produced more than 1 million gallons of wine in 2013, according to the Department of the Treasury's Alcohol and Tobacco Tax and Trade Bureau:

- California: 728,939,759 gallons
- Washington: 34,144,441
- New York: 27,150,759
- Pennsylvania: 10,272,127
- Oregon: 7,948,408
- Vermont: 4,315,420
- Ohio: 3,277,838
- Kentucky: 2,241,527
- Michigan: 2,180,359
- Florida: 2,026,230
- Tennessee: 1,144,283
- North Carolina: 1,351,975
- New Jersey: 1,329,932
- Virginia: 1,261,104
- Missouri: 1,250,654
- Indiana: 1,100,872

Tours of the winery and vineyard are offered several times throughout the week. Reservations can be made online at www.fiorelliwinery.com/tours.

If you try a wine you like, be sure to buy a bottle before you leave. Rosa Fiorelli's wines, which have been winning awards since 1999, are not sold in any stores yet.

"Our goal is to expand and to get into distribution," Sal said.

The winery offers special events each month in its pavilion and courtyard, which combined provides about 2,000 square feet for entertaining.

If You Go

Where: Rosa Fiorelli Winery & Vineyard, 4250 County Road 675 E, Bradenton
Contact: 941-322-0976 or www.fiorelliwinery.com

Siesta Key Rum, Sarasota

The name Troy Roberts doesn't exactly conjure up images of a cold fruity drink sweating in your hand as the sun sets and steel drums lull away the day's stress.

The name Troy Roberts sounds like someone enjoying one of those drinks.

The name Troy Roberts, however, has become THE name in the rum world. Ya mon!

Troy started his company Drum Circle Distilling in 2007, and opened the Sarasota distillery the following year. Soon thereafter, Troy's Siesta Key Rums became bottled magic.

"Troy Roberts' Sarasota distillery is, right now, the best in America," wrote the Caribbean Journal in its 2015 Best American Rum list. "There's a reason his limited edition rums sell out in hours, the lines get longer and longer and the distribution keeps expanding. Siesta Key's signature spiced blend is a gold-medal knockout that isn't just the best in America — it's better than any in the Caribbean, too."

Ya mon!

Drum Circle Distilling's rums include Siesta Key Toasted Coconut, Siesta Key Spiced, Distiller's Reserve Spiced, Beer Barrel Finish Spiced, Siesta Key Silver and Siesta Key Gold.

The spiced rums have won a lot of awards. All three spiced rums were named among the 2015 RumXP Best in Class and Gold Medal winners. Caribbean Journal named 'Siesta Key Distillers Reserve Spiced Rum' the Spiced Rum of the Year... multiple years in a row.

"It's getting to the point where we might have to change the name of this category to Siesta Key Rum of the Year," the Journal wrote in 2014. "Three years, three wins by the boutique distillery in Sarasota. ... This year, distiller Troy Roberts unveiled an even smaller-batch rum, Distillers Reserve, a solera-aged rum that achieves something almost unheard of in the spiced category: it's so good you can drink it neat."

Many restaurants and stores in more than a dozen states, along with Disney World, now offer various kinds of Siesta Key rums. "We have people from all over the world trying to buy our rum," he said.

Troy, founder, CEO and head distiller, offers free tours of his Sarasota distillery on Tuesdays and Saturdays. The tours also include a stop in the tasting room, where free samples are provided and bottles are sold. Ya mon!

"I'm making rum while we speak," he said during a tour.

Troy's family began vacationing in Siesta Key when he was young, and they eventually moved to the area when he was 14. "He spent the first part of his life being a beach bum in Sarasota, a ski bum in Denver, a sail bum in Santa Cruz, and a frozen yogurt store owner in Portland, Oregon," his bio states.

Troy worked as a director of product management for Compuware Corp., and founded several auto-related websites, which he sold in order to return to his beach roots.

"The name was a hard thing to choose," he said. He selected Siesta Key Rum because "it reflected what I wanted the rum to be: beachy, but not Daytona beachy."

He has succeeded. Siesta Key is one of the best beaches in the world, and the local rum is living up to its name.

His secret: quality over quantity.

If You Go

Where: Drum Circle Distilling, 2212 Industrial Blvd., Sarasota

More info: 941-702-8143 or *www.drumcircledistilling.com/ drum-circle-distilling.html*

"We make it with real spices," he said of his spiced rums. "Most spiced rum is not made with real spices." Also, "we use molasses… we use the good stuff."

The Siesta Key Toasted Coconut Rum is made with real, shredded, toasted coconut, Troy said.

"We cannot make enough of that stuff," Troy said. "There was like a three-hour line for that last December."

Troy offers detailed explanations as to how the rums are made, aged, stored and bottled during the tours of the impeccably clean facility. "Each week, we're producing between 1,200 and 1,500 bottles," he said. "We write the batch number by hand on every bottle. … Our fingerprints are on every bottle."

Troy's business is a family business as well. His wife Nanci works as a manager in the tasting room, as does his mother Shari. In fact, Shari and Troy designed the first Siesta Key Rum label. And Troy's father Jim, well, he seems to do it all.

"He is the guy who can fix things when nobody else can," his bio states on the website. "He can also build most anything, including our barrel racks and tasting room."

Troy's tours may have more than 50 people, as ours did, but it still felt intimate and personal. Questions were welcomed, as was interaction. And no one went home thirsty. Ya mon!

Snook Haven, Venice

At the end of a long dirt road in Venice is a place where the palm trees sip from the Myakka River and the fish compete in jumping contests.

It's a place where the music is playing, the meat is smoking and the cold beer is flowing.

It's Snook Haven, an Old-Florida restaurant/music venue/natural sedative. Heck, being at Snook Haven is as relaxing as lounging in a recliner that has a refrigerated cup holder. Yes, I just used the word "heck." That's what happens at Snook Haven.

Snook Haven offers indoor and outdoor dining. Some of the outdoor dining overlooks the Myakka River, while a larger portion of the seating is located near the entertainment area.

Live Like A Tourist ... **During Happy Hour**

The entertainment changes daily, so check out the calendar on Snook Haven's website, *www.snookhaven.com.*

And the food is not ordinary "bar" food.

Two large smokers flavor meats for 10 to 15 hours.

The large menu includes a "Pick 2" option, allowing diners to select two kinds of meat and two side dishes for $13.95. I chose the pulled pork (super moist) and smoked turkey (very flavorful), along with macaroni and cheese (don't judge, I'm a mac-n-cheese nut) and the crisp homemade chips. Everything was fantastic. The meal also was a very hearty portion (a take-home box may be needed).

Even the barbecue sauces are homemade. The three flavors offered include sweet, original and whiskey, which has a spicy kick to it.

In addition to the great food, spectacular views and regular entertainment, there also are organized activities available, such as cornhole tournaments and kids nights.

Kayakers also are welcome to use the Snook Haven as a launch for exploring the Myakka River, which Hollywood once used to film "Revenge of the Killer Turtles."

Fear not, I saw no killer turtles during my afternoon at Snook Haven — a trip I plan to repeat soon.

If You Go

Where: Snook Haven,
5000 E. Venice Ave., Venice
More info: 941-485-7221
Tips: Check out the
entertainment calendar on
Snook Haven's website,
www.snookhaven.com

Live Like A Tourist ... **During Happy Hour**

Wicked Dolphin, Cape Coral

Free booze.

I thought that might get your attention.

I was afraid to write "good free booze," because if I had, some of you would be calling in sick. Rest assured, the good free booze is available on Saturdays as well.

So enough stalling, the good free booze is available by touring the Wicked Dolphin Artisan Rum distillery in Cape Coral. That's right, there is a local rum distillery in Lee County. And it's not a tiny, creepy, dirty warehouse producing a few sketchy bottles of cheap rum. This is a beautiful, exceptionally clean, creatively painted distillery that produces three kinds of rums, which are available in more than 2,000 locations such as Publix, Winn-Dixie and ABC Fine Wine & Spirits. Sam's Club is the newest addition in this area.

"You should be able to find us," said Jordan Boyd, Wicked Dolphin tour guide.

Or, you can drive to Cape Coral and tour the distillery while buying beautiful bottles of Wicked Dolphin Silver, Florida Spiced and Coconuts rums. Free tours are offered at various times and days.

Owner JoAnn Elardo started Wicked Dolphin in 2012. JoAnn, who designed the logo and the bottle, picked the name after a dolphin experience. She lives on the Caloosahatchee River, where dolphins regularly swim by — aggravating her dogs. At 3 a.m. one day, JoAnn woke up to a dog growling. She thought her home had been broken into, but her husband said, "It's that wicked dolphin. He's back."

Thus the name was born, as was one of the fastest-growing rum brands.

"We have a lot of serious rum connoisseurs that like us and spread the word," JoAnn said.

JoAnn works with her nephew, Dan Termini, who is the master distiller. "The whole thing about Wicked Dolphin and our brand: We're Florida," she said.

During the tour, you will learn that Wicked Dolphin uses Florida sugar in addition to other local products. "Anything that grows down here, the guys will experiment with," said Chris Hein, in charge of retail operations and special events for Wicked Dolphin.

Live Like A Tourist ... **During Happy Hour**

Jordan first described Wicked Dolphin's products, while guests sipped a mixed drink made from cranberry juice, pineapple juice and Wicked Dolphin's Silver and Coconut rums.

Silver Rum was Wicked Dolphin's first. It ages for at least a year in a barrel used once by a bourbon maker.

Wicked Dolphin takes great care in making its rums, which includes a process that removes "bad alcohol." They use the bad alcohol, which smells disgustingly harsh and pungent, for cleaning. Removing the bad alcohol is the difference between good alcohol and bad alcohol, Jordan said.

"You are drinking a little nail polish remover or paint thinner," Jordan said. "That's why you get a bad headache when you drink cheap alcohol."

Florida Spiced Rum, also aged for 1 to 1 ½ years, "is distinctively Florida with notes of Florida oranges and honey with a creamy vanilla undertone and a spicy finish," states the website.

The Coconut Rum is the newest of the rums and it's made with coconut water.

"Our coconut is brand new," JoAnn said. "We've been selling like crazy. It's just hitting the stores."

Chris called it their "labor of love." "The guys worked on this for about two years," she said.

If You Go

Where: Wicked Dolphin, 131 S.W. 3rd Place, Cape Coral
More info: 239-242-5244 or *http://wickeddolphinrum.com*

The Spirits Business named Wicked Dolphin among the top 10 American craft rum brands. "Located a few miles away from Florida's fertile sugarcane fields is Wicked Dolphin Distillery, which produces a range of award-winning artisan rums," states the article. "The distillery's Silver Rum is handcrafted in small batches using a copper pot still, and then blended with rum aged in a Kentucky Bourbon barrel."

Wicked Dolphin also has tapped into the increasingly popular moonshine business by creating three "Rumshines," in the flavors of strawberry, blueberry and apple.

The distillers are constantly working on new products, and the next one likely will be Florida Gold Rum, JoAnn said.

"There's a specific timing of flavors," Jordan said. "We go through a lot of experiments."

The experimenters also have been making barbecue sauces, which are made with rum. Hot sauces also is available in three flavors, Habanero, Serrano and Cayenne. These products, along the rums, T-shirts, glasses and other goods are available in Wicked Dolphin's store, where the free tour begins and ends.

Yuengling, Tampa

Mmm ... beer.

Famous writers, actors, musicians and philosophers have talked about the gift that is beer for centuries.

"Without question, the greatest invention in the history of mankind is beer. Oh, I grant you the wheel was also a fine invention, but the wheel does not go nearly as well with pizza." — Writer Dave Barry, who should order a Leinenkugel Berry Weiss because that would just be awesome — Barry-Berry.

"Beer is proof that God loves us and wants us to be happy." — Benjamin Franklin. I mean, really, how can you argue with him?

"Beer — now there's a temporary solution." — Philosopher Homer... Simpson.

And what's better than beer? No, not wine. Free beer!

So gas up the car and let's go to the Yuengling Brewery in Tampa, where you can tour the facility and taste free beer.

Mmm ... free beer.

Yuengling offers free tours six days a week, but it's best to go Monday through Thursday, when most of the plant is fully operating.

Yuengling, America's oldest brewery, which started in 1829 in Pottsville, Pa., has three plants in the United States. Two are located in Pennsylvania, and the

212

Live Like A Tourist ... **During Happy Hour**

Where: Yuengling Brewery, 11111 N. 30th St, Tampa

Tips: Must wear closed shoes (meaning no sandals, flip-flops, Crocs, etc.)

More info: *www.yuengling.com/breweries/tampa*

one in Tampa, which originally opened in 1958 by Schlitz. Later it became the brewery for Stroh's, Pabst, Stroh's again and then Yuengling in 1999.

Hospitality Manager Elizabeth Maroney provided a lot of information during a tour, which took about 45 minutes. The tour can last longer if there are a lot of questions, but apparently our group was more interested in getting back to the free beer.

Elizabeth will take guests around and explain how the beer is made, where the ingredients come from, etc.

Here are a few fun facts: The grains originate in the Midwest and arrive via rail car. Yuengling's Oktoberfest beer contains barley from Germany. The Yuengling plant can fill up to 900 bottles a minute, though it generally operates at about 850 bottles a minute. That's a lot of beer. The bottles also go through an X-ray machine, which can tell if the caps are properly applied and if the appropriate amount of liquid is in each bottle. And, beer freezes at 28 degrees.

The tour includes a trip into the lab, where the experienced chemists can provide a lot of detailed information that went right over my head — and no, it's not because I had already started drinking free beer. I have a bachelor of arts degree with an emphasis on arts, not science.

Yuengling has seven regular beers: Premium, Porter, Black & Tan, Lager, Light Lager, Chesterfield Ale and Light. The company also offers seasonal beers such as Bock, Summer Wheat and Oktoberfest.

There is a gift shop at the brewery, where attractive Yuengling T-shirts, hats and other souvenirs can be purchased.

A visit to Yuengling isn't an all-day adventure. I imagine they'd kick you out after a while. Busch Gardens, Adventure Island and MOSI (Museum of Science and Industry) are all nearby and can be worked in with a trip to Yuengling for a free tour. And don't forget the free beer ... Mmm ... beer.

CPSIA information can be obtained at www.ICGtesting.com
Printed in the USA
LVOW06s0957090116

469167LV00003B/4/P